Longman Self-help g

Children and the Law

*Young people
and their rights*

Maggie Rae

Longman

Longman Group UK Limited,
Longman House, Burnt Mill, Harlow,
Essex CM20 2JE, England
and Associated Companies throughout the world.

First published 1986

Rae, Maggie
Children and the law.—(Longman self-help guides)
    1. Children—Legal status, laws, etc.—England
I. Title
344.202′87   KD3305
ISBN 0–582–89334–8

Set in Monophoto Plantin 10/11 point
Printed in Great Britain
by Butler & Tanner Ltd, Frome and London

ABOUT THE AUTHOR

Maggie Rae is a solicitor in private practice in North London. She specializes in family law. She has written extensively on the subject, and also lectures from time to time. She lives in East London with her cohabitee Alan Haworth and three delinquent cats.

Contents

Acknowledgements

This book could not have been written without the help of a large number of people, including:

Andy Hall
Henry Hodge
Holly Rae
Sue Shutter

Special thanks are also due to the staff at the Children's Legal Centre both for agreeing to look at the text and for their work in promoting the interests of the child as a person. This has helped to shape the tone of this book and, I hope, to make it more relevant to children themselves.
Finally I would like to pay particular tribute to the help given by Kathy Swift, Liz Wilhyde, and the editors at the Longman Group whose patience and encouragement were endless and invaluable. Mistakes, of course, remain my own.

Maggie Rae
May 1986

To Holly Rae

Introduction

From any standpoint, the law as it relates to children is controversial, illogical and badly understood. Reform is long overdue.

Much criticism has been made of the haphazard way in which children acquire different rights. Why, for example, should a child be able to marry at 16, but not vote until 18? Why can't there be one set of rules about children's banking rights, instead of several? The law in this area is clearly a mess.

All sorts of curious and arcane rules govern other aspects of children's lives. Contracts entered into by children, for instance, are held to be binding if they concern 'necessaries'. What is 'necessary'? The law is unable to say with any certainty. The suggestion made by the Children's Legal Centre that only contracts made by children over a certain age should be enforceable seems to have fallen on deaf ears, despite having the virtues of clarity and logic on its side.

These are just some of the areas in which the law is confused or inconsistent. A more serious and substantial criticism is that English law gives children very little access to the courts at all. Children can participate in care proceedings, but that is almost the only time that they do, except when they are charged with criminal offences. And the new custodianship legislation allows them very little say in cases which decide their legal status. Children involved in custody disputes could be forgiven for thinking that the courts view them merely as pawns in an adult game, so limited are their rights to express their views.

Reforms are obviously necessary to allow children more opportunity to participate in legal procedures that will drastically affect their lives. However, calls for a children's ombudsman to safeguard and promote the rights of children have so far met with no governmental response.

This book aims to give a straightforward account of the law as it stands, warts and all. It is for children and those whose task is to help and advise them.

Using the Law

Children can become involved in the court system in many different ways. They can be the subject of custody disputes between their parents or of care proceedings brought by the local authority. They can be involved in other sorts of cases, for example, because they have been injured as a result of someone else's negligence. They can also be charged with criminal offences in their own right.

All of these types of cases are dealt with in different ways and often by different courts in the English court system. The laws that assign cases to particular courts are, in cases involving children in particular, a mess.

An unfortunate feature of English law is that children have very few rights of access to the court system. There are few proceedings where a child can apply to the court—care proceedings are a notable exception. In other proceedings a child can start court proceedings but will need an adult's assistance. Actions for damages are an example of this.

In many circumstances a child does not even have a right to be heard in court proceedings that may drastically affect his or her life. Custody and custodianship proceedings fall into this group.

The following section describes the main features of the various courts in which cases concerning children are dealt with.

The juvenile court

The juvenile court is a special type of magistrates' court which only deals with cases involving children under 17 (for criminal proceedings) or under 18 (for care proceedings). It deals with both criminal and civil proceedings. Juvenile courts are designed to be less formal and intimidating than adult magistrates' courts.

Magistrates

Cases in the juvenile court are usually decided by a bench of three
magistrates selected from the magistrates who sit in the area in
which the juvenile court is situated. They are supposed to be
especially qualified to deal with juvenile cases. They serve on the
juvenile panel for three years at a time. In Inner London the panel
is nominated by the Lord Chancellor. Every juvenile court bench
is supposed to include at least one woman.

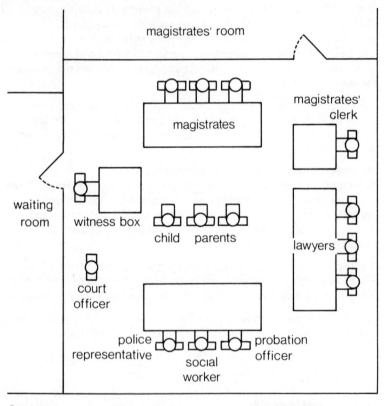

Layout

The physical layout of the court is different from that of a
magistrates' court for adults. The magistrates' court
normally has a dock, in which the person accused of the offence
is required to sit. It is usually fairly large, mainly because so many
of these courts were built at the turn of the century and may be
quite intimidating. By contrast, juvenile courts are usually smaller

and are furnished with tables and chairs instead of the more
formal benches of the magistrates' court.

Usually the court expects at least one of the child's parents to be
present. The child will be able to sit next to them, at the front of
the court. The precise layout may vary from court to court.

Other people allowed in court

Cases are heard in private. Members of the press can come into
the court but there are restrictions on what they may report.
Generally they cannot report a case in any way that would identify
the child. The court or the Secretary of State can waive this
requirement but only if it is in the interests of the child to do so.

Apart from the child, the parents, the magistrates, the magistrates'
clerk and any members of the press the only other people who
can be present iin the court are:

- the lawyers concerned with the case

- court officers such as the court usher

- the representative of the local education authority

- anybody else that the court specially authorizes to be present

In practice, there are often a great many people in the juvenile
court when a case is heard. The local authority will usually send
a social worker and there may be someone from the education and
probation services, too. Witnesses in the case may also sit in court,
but usually only after they have given their evidence.

Procedure

The procedure in the juvenile court is designed to be simple and
comprehensible. The law itself is so complicated that this aim is
difficult to achieve. However, as far as possible, the court should
conduct its proceedings using straightforward language. In
criminal cases the charge should be explained to the child in simple
language. The child should then be asked whether or not they
admit the offence.

Anyone giving evidence in any court is usually required to take an
oath, which varies according to the religion or otherwise of the
person giving the evidence. There is a special form of

oath which is used in the juvenile court and which is meant to be more straightforward. It is called the promissory oath because it begins with the words 'I promise' rather than the words 'I swear'.

As in any magistrates' court, evidence is given verbally. There is very little provision for evidence to be given in writing. There are some exceptions to this.

Evidence of criminal convictions can be given by production of what is called a 'memorandum of conviction', which is an extract from the Register of Convictions held by magistrates' and juvenile courts. This can be relevant in care proceedings. It may be needed, for example, where the local authority says that one parent has been convicted of an offence relevant to the proceedings.

In care proceedings a child's school attendance can be crucial and this can be proved to the court by a form of certificate from the education department.

In care proceedings medical reports can also be admitted in the form of written evidence, as long as they deal only with the person's physical or mental condition. A certificate which expresses an opinion as to how an injury was caused would not be admissible and the doctor would have to attend and give evidence.

Reports from *guardians ad litem*, social workers and others are also allowed, but only after the case has been heard and proved, and the magistrates are deciding what, if any, order or sentence to make.

The magistrates' court

Magistrates' courts deal mainly with cases involving adults. However, they can deal with certain cases involving children, or which affect them:

- a case where a juvenile is charged with a criminal offence together with an adult must be heard in magistrates' court (see page 176)

- custody proceedings

● some proceedings concerning the maintenance of children (see pages 34 and 37)

● adoption proceedings (see page 47)

● affiliation proceedings (see page 37)

● custodianship cases (see page 79)

Magistrates' courts deal with both criminal and civil cases. The procedure in both is largely the same although there are differences in the way that family cases are handled.

Magistrates

The court is usually presided over by three lay magistrates, although criminal cases can be decided by one stipendiary magistrate. A stipendiary magistrate is a qualified lawyer who is employed full-time as a magistrate. These magistrates are fairly common in London but not elsewhere.

When the magistrates' court is dealing with family matters, such as custody or affiliation, it will normally consist of three magistrates, even if one of them is a stipendiary magistrate. Magistrates' courts often refer to family cases as domestic cases.

Procedure

Evidence has to be given orally and cannot usually be given by a written statement, although reports are received in domestic or family cases.

In criminal cases magistrates' courts are open to the public and press. Press reporting of young people is restricted in the same way as in the juvenile court. Family cases should be heard in private.

The county court

County courts exist for every area in England and Wales. Cases are heard by judges or registrars. Judges and registrars are trained lawyers and must fulfil stringent requirements as to their experience and good character before being appointed.

County courts do not deal with criminal offences. They do, however, deal with a great many types of civil cases, many of which concern children. These include cases on adoption, custody, custodianship, guardianship and some cases for damages where a child is suing or being sued for an injury. Most divorce cases are dealt with by the county court. They also handle cases to do with racial and sexual discrimination.

Procedure

Proceedings are started by filing a written document with the court setting out the orders which are sought and the justification for seeking them.

There are two main types of document. One is called a 'particulars of claim' and the other is called an 'originating application'. Adoption and custody cases are started by an originating application while a case dealing with damages for personal injuries suffered is started by a 'particulars of claim'.

The county courts normally hear oral evidence but there are provisions which enable written evidence to be submitted; in some cases this is insisted upon. Written evidence is normally provided in the form of an affidavit, which is a statement of the person's evidence which has been sworn before a solicitor. County courts do not have the same restrictions on other written documents as magistrates' and juvenile courts. Medical reports and other kinds of written documents will often be used in a case.

Family cases in county courts are heard in private. The press is not admitted.

The High Court

The High Court is divided into three divisions: the Family Division, the Queen's Bench Division and the Chancery Division. The Family Division is mostly concerned with cases about children. However, the Queen's Bench Division and the Chancery Division can also deal with children's cases.

The Family Division of the High Court has the power to hear cases on custody, adoption and guardianship that concern children. It can hear appeals in cases concerning children from the magistrates' courts. The High Court is also the only court in the country that can deal with wardship cases (see page 74).

In the Family Division of the High Court evidence is normally given in written form, by means of an affidavit on which the person giving the evidence can be asked questions. Family cases are heard in private.

The Queen's Bench Division and the Chancery Division of the High Court can deal with certain children's cases, for example, those where a child is sued or being sued as a result of an injury suffered. These courts may also hear cases involving the interpretation of legislation—or rules that affect children. If a local authority is alleged to have behaved improperly to a child in its care the case might come before the Queen's Bench Division. Recently, when the Department of Health and Social Security's regulations regarding board and lodging payments for young people were challenged, the case was heard by the Queen's Bench Division. Mrs Gillick's case regarding contraceptive advice to those under 16 was also first heard in the Queen's Bench Division.

The High Court sits in London but has District Registries or branches all over the country. Judges from all three divisions of the High Court go round the country to hear cases.

The crown court

Crown courts are almost exclusively concerned with criminal cases. These are normally dealt with by a judge, who sits with a jury of 12 men and women to decide the case. Children and young people are not normally entitled to be tried by a judge and jury but must have their case heard by the juvenile court. There are exceptions to this, however (see page 176).

At the moment, the crown court hears appeals against care proceedings in the juvenile court. In such cases, the appeal is heard by a crown court judge sitting with two juvenile court magistrates. They will hear the case again and decide whether or not to make the order requested.

The crown court also hears appeals from criminal proceedings in the juvenile courts and applications for bail where the juvenile court has refused it.

The Court of Appeal

This court hears appeals from crown courts, the High Court and county courts. Cases are decided by three or sometimes two senior judges. Some of these cases, for example, wardship and adoption cases, concern children.

The House of Lords

The House of Lords is the highest court in the United Kingdom. It hears appeals from the Court of Appeal. The judges in the House of Lords are Law Lords and cases are usually heard by five of them.

Although not many cases come to the House of Lords to be decided, the House of Lords has decided a number of important ones involving children. Recently it gave the final decision on the case brought by Mrs Gillick regarding the availability of contraceptive advice and treatment to girls under 16.

The European Court

The European Court sits in Strasbourg. Anybody of any age who believes that a basic right set out in the European Convention has been violated can complain to the European Commission on Human Rights here.

A complaint to the Commission can only be made by those who have themselves been affected by violation of a right. They must also have tried all domestic remedies, which often involves appealing to the House of Lords.

Proceedings at the Commission take a long time. If the Commission decides that the complaint is admissible it will investigate the case and attempt to reach a friendly settlement. If this does not work, the Commission will then provide a report and give a legal opinion which then go before the Committee of Ministers representing all the member states of the Council of Europe. The case can then go, in certain circumstances, to the European Court.

This court consists of seven judges, it normally sits in public and always gives its judgments in public. It can award compensation. Countries who have signed the Convention, and this includes Britain, have agreed to respect decisions of the Committee of Ministers and the court.

The European Commission and Court have been involved in several cases concerning children. In some, this has led to the British government taking action. For example, when the Children's Legal Centre alleged that locking children up in care was in breach of the European Convention the British government changed the law and brought in secure accommodation orders (see page 70).

A less successful result occurred when the British government was held to be in breach of the European Convention by not respecting parents' objections to corporal punishment in state schools. The government introduced legislation to bring itself within the scope of the European Court decision but this was defeated in Parliament and has not subsequently been re-introduced. Other cases concerning children are pending with the European Commission and Court at the present time.

Legal representation

Getting help

Children's law is complicated and many lawyers are not familiar with all of it. Some of the problems with which young people are faced need a solicitor—for example, those where a person is charged with a criminal offence or held at a police station. Other situations may be better handled by different means. For example, if a young person has a dispute with their social worker, a lawyer may not be able to do much. Likewise, young people have few rights to initiate court action and so cannot easily pursue many grievances in the way that adults can. Seeking advice from specialist organizations can be helpful. Cost ought not to deter young people from seeking advice (see page 13).

Choosing a solicitor

Many people are understandably wary about going to see a solicitor. Many solicitors are not specialists in cases concerning children and a child who wishes to take court action, or who is being brought before the courts, should try and ensure that they are representted by someone who is knowledgeable.

The local Citizens' Advice Bureau can often advise which solicitors in the area are likely to be experienced in the particular kind of case. Sometimes youth workers or social workers can also advise on the choice of a solicitor. The Children's Legal Centre may be able to help and may be able to refer a young person to a specialist lawyer.

Special arrangements apply concerning care cases in the juvenile courts. In order to represent a child in care proceedings a solicitor should have special expertise and training in such work. The court has a list of solicitors in the area who have that expertise. Often, however, the solicitor in care proceedings will not be chosen by the child but by the *Guardian ad litem* (see page 60).

The Official Solicitor

The Official Solicitor is appointed by the Lord Chancellor's department. He is a qualified solicitor and in charge of an office in London which is staffed by solicitors and others. The Official Solicitor has many areas of responsibility, including the representation of children in certain types of cases.

The Official Solicitor will usually represent children if they have been made parties in wardship proceedings. He can also represent them if they have been made parties in custody proceedings in the High Court or the county court. He is not obliged to represent children but will normally do so if asked by the court.

The Official Solicitor represents some children in cases where they are suing for damages because of injuries they have suffered and there is no adult able to act as the child's *Guardian ad litem*. The Official Solicitor also acts as the child's *Guardian ad litem* in High Court adoption cases (see page 49).

In family matters the Official Solicitor cannot start proceedings and so a child who wishes to start wardship proceedings will need to find another adult to act as *Guardian ad litem*. In such a case it is most important to obtain help from a knowledgeable solicitor.

Legal aid

Legal aid in criminal proceedings

Children and young people charged with criminal offences can instruct a solicitor themselves. Criminal legal aid is available to defend prosecutions and to apply for bail in the crown court.

Legal aid applications are made on a form which is available from the court or from the solicitor. The application will be decided on the financial eligibility of the person concerned and whether it is in the interests of justice to grant legal aid.

In order to decide financial eligibility a 'statement of means' form will have to be filled in. This is normally filled in by the parents of someone under 16; over 16, by the young person. If a child is in care the parents' means do not need to be divulged; the child's income will be considered on its own. If legal aid is granted, the court can order that a contribution should be paid.

The court should grant legal aid if:

- the young person is in danger of a custodial sentence
- they are in danger of losing their job
- a substantial question of law is involved or the case is a complex one
- the young person cannot follow the proceedings because of a disability or cannot understand or speak English
- the case involves expert cross-examination of a prosecution witness

Apart from these considerations there are certain specific cases where the court should grant legal aid as long as a person's means are fairly limited. These are where:

- young people have been refused bail

- the court is considering sentencing young people to detention centre, youth custody, custody for life or detention for long periods of time

- and the court is considering making a care order as a sentence for a criminal offence, or a charge and control condition suspending or preventing a child returning home when in care (see page 185), or an order restricting the child's liberty while in care if the young person is committed to trial at the crown court for murder

Legal aid in care proceedings

The child is always a party in care proceedings and can apply for legal aid. The legal aid forms are the same as those for criminal cases. Legal aid is normally granted (see page 60).

Legal aid in parental rights resolutions

Different legal aid regulations apply here. The child is not automatically a party to the proceedings but, if made a party, legal aid can be applied for.

Legal aid in civil proceedings

In civil proceedings young people under 18 are held by the law to be at a disadvantage. They must be represented by an adult, called the 'next friend' if the young person is instituting the proceedings, or a *Guardian ad litem* if the young person is being sued. These people must act through a solicitor and can apply for legal aid. Legal aid forms are available from solicitors, or from the Law Society. Local Law Societies exist for each region. Their addresses are in the telephone book.

Although children cannot apply for legal aid on their own account their resources will be considered. These will be added to the resources of anyone who is legally responsible for maintaining the child and with whom the child is living, unless that person has a contrary interest in the case, or in other exceptional circumstances. If a young person is in care or living away from home, only his or her resources will usually be assessed. The financial resources of the *Guardian ad litem* or 'next friend' are not taken into account unless they are responsible for the maintenance of the child and living with the child. A young person who is suing for money owed in the county court does not have to act through an adult and can apply for legal aid on his or her own account.

Financial resources are assessed by the DHSS and this can take some time. Applications for legal aid normally take five or six weeks, or sometimes longer. In emergencies, however, the Law Society can grant emergency legal aid. A young person who thinks their case is urgent should ask their solicitor about this.

Legal advice

The legal aid scheme includes a provision known as the Green Form Scheme under which people can get cheap or free advice and practical help from a solicitor on any matter of English law. This is subject to two conditions.

The most important one affecting young people is that those under 16 cannot usually sign the legal aid form themselves. However, a parent or anybody helping the young person may sign the form on their behalf. Usually the permission of the Law Society will be needed.

A solicitor can apply to the local Law Society Committee for permission to accept a Green Form signed by a person under 16. The Law Society should grant permission if it feels that it is reasonable in the circumstances that the child should receive advice and assistance. Young people over 16 can apply for Green Form assistance in the same way as adults.

The second requirement is that whoever signs the Green Form must come within the financial eligibility requirements laid down by the Law Society. The Green Form is signed in the solicitor's office. The solicitor then works out from a form provided by the Law Society whether or not the person is eligible.

Fixed-fee interviews

Many solicitors provide fixed-fee interviews. This scheme gives a person half an hour's advice for no more than £5. It is worth asking solicitors when making the appointment whether or not they give fixed-fee interviews and whether or not they do work under the Green Form and legal aid schemes.

Children and their Parents

Because children cannot look after themselves the law places this responsibility on their parents. This means that the parents have the right to make all the major decisions regarding the upbringing of their children. Gradually, as the children get older, they acquire rights to make decisions for themselves.

Until this century it was fathers who had most of the rights over their children. This has now changed. In the case of legitimate children the law presumes that both parents share custody. In the case of an illegitimate child, the mother has sole legal custody. These presumptions can be overturned by the courts who have wide powers to resolve disputes between parents.

Increasingly, the law allows people other than parents to apply to the courts for custody. There is, however, almost no provision for children to apply to the courts if they are dissatisfied about the way in which they are being looked after (but see Chapter 5).

The law does not specify parental rights in any detail but leaves it largely to common sense. Nor does the law state with any clarity the age at which children can make their own decisions.

Over the years the rights of parents have been the subject of judicial comment. In 1969 Lord Denning assessed the position thus: 'Parents' rights are dwindling rights.' Parental power, he said, 'starts with a right of control and ends with little more than advice'. This was echoed in the House of Lords' decision in the Gillick case in 1985 when Lord Fraser said, 'Most wise parents relax their controls gradually as the child develops and encourage him or her to become increasingly independent.' In the same case Lord Scarman said, 'Parental rights are derived from parental duty and exist only so long as they are needed for the protection of the person and property of the child.'

Parental rights and duties

A child reaches the 'age of majority' at 18, at which time most parental rights and duties cease. The rights and duties described in this section are shared equally by married parents. In the case of an illegitimate child, these rights are the mother's alone.

Name

In general, it is the parents who have the right to choose the child's name. Only in exceptional circumstances can a parent change a child's name subsequently. This is dealt with in more detail in Chapter 10.

Possession of the child

The law starts with the presumption that parents have the right to look after their children, either by themselves or by making arrangements with other people. They are given a wide measure of discretion. They can determine the child's diet, decide how the child is to be dressed and housed. They have a great deal of control over how their children spend their time. However, the right to look after the child and make these decisions about upbringing also carries with it duties. There are many steps that can be taken if parental care is not of a reasonable standard.

The standard is not specified in law but clearly does not allow parents, for example, to undernourish their children and prevent their proper development, or to clothe them in a wholly inadequate way. Parents can be prosecuted if they abandon their child or fail to give the child the basic necessities for life.

In particular, a parent who acts cruelly to a child under 16 years old can be prosecuted for assaulting, ill-treating, neglecting or abandoning a child, or for exposing the child to harm which is likely to cause the child unnecessary suffering or injury to health. This can include refusing to allow the child to have proper medical treatment.

Prosecutions of parents are not common except in cases of severe physical ill-treatment. If a parent fails to look after a child properly it is more likely that the child will be made the subject of care proceedings (see page 57).

The right of the parent to have custody and care of the child is recognized by the law which has provided that people who abduct or take a child away from the person who has custody can be prosecuted (see page 32). It is also open to the parent to apply to the court for an order protecting their right to custody of their child in either wardship proceedings or custody proceedings (see pages 30 and 74).

Discipline

Parents have the right to discipline their children and to say how their children should behave. There are wide variations in what is thought to be acceptable. Some parents never use any form of physical punishment whereas others use it frequently. The law does not prevent parents inflicting physical punishment on their children, but the punishment has to be 'reasonable' by commonly accepted standards in this country. A parent from a country where harsh physical punishment is acceptable will be expected to moderate their standards while they are living in this country.

A parent who inflicts excessive punishment or severely punishes a child for no good reason may find themselves prosecuted for cruelty, and have their child taken into care.

Medical treatment

A child under 16 cannot normally consent to medical or dental treatment. This whole area of parental control has recently come under review by the House of Lords during the case brought by Mrs Gillick against her Local Area Health Authority.

The dispute concerned the giving of contraceptive advice and treatment to girls under 16. In the Gillick case Lord Fraser specified conditions for a doctor giving such advice to a girl without informing her parents. He said that doctors would be justified in doing so if satisfied 'that the girl (although under 16 years of age) will understand his advice; that he cannot persuade her to inform her parents or to allow him to inform the parents that she is seeking contraceptive advice; that she is very likely to be having or continue having sexual intercourse without contraceptive treatment; that unless she receives contraceptive advice or treatment her physical or mental health or both are likely to suffer; and that her best interests require him to give her contraceptive advice, treatment or both without the parental consent'. At the time of writing the DHSS is expected to bring out guidelines to doctors reflecting the Gillick decision.

The right of parents to consent to medical treatment can be overruled by the courts. An example was a case where a court was asked to forbid a child to be sterilized despite the fact that the child's mother wished her to have that operation. In another case the court ordered that a severely handicapped child have a life-saving operation against the wishes of the parents.

Parents who have refused consent for their children to have blood transfusions have also been overruled by the courts. Where a child's life is in danger doctors can treat the child without the parents' consent. Parents who fail to ensure that their children receive proper medical treatment can find that their child is made the subject of care proceedings.

Education

Parents have the right to decide how their child should be educated. This right, however, is subject to the law which provides that a child of compulsory school age must receive efficient full-time education which is appropriate to the child's age, ability and aptitude. Parents who do not ensure that this duty is met can be prosecuted and their children taken into care.

Within these limits, parents have a wide choice to decide exactly how their child should be educated, at school or otherwise, and in the state or private systems. The child has virtually no rights to choose what type of education he or she receives. The respective roles of parents and education authorities is dealt with in more detail in Chapter 6.

Religion

Parents can choose whether to bring their child up in a particular religious faith but are not obliged to do so. However, the law will act to protect the child if a parent's religious beliefs are harmful to the child.

Difficulties have arisen where the religious beliefs of parents can result in positive harm to a child. Jehovah's Witnesses, for example, refuse to allow blood transfusions. More recently the practice of female circumcision practised by some religions has led to intervention by the government.

If parents cannot agree about the child's religious upbringing this can also be decided by the courts. Normally the courts are reluctant to change a religious belief which the child has already adopted. Again, children have no rights under the law to stop parents bringing them up in a particular religious faith.

Access

The parents' right to care and possession of their child means that they have considerable freedom to decide who they allow the child to mix with. People apart from the parents have very few rights to see the child.

Problems can arise if grandparents, for example, are not allowed to see their grandchild. There are limited ways in which grandparents can now intervene and ask the court to grant them access, particularly in custody and separation proceedings brought in the magistrates' or county courts (see page 30). Otherwise, grandparents or other relatives would have to show that the child was positively being harmed by the refusal of access before the courts would consider interfering with the parents' discretion.

When parents separate, courts normally give the parent who does not have custody access to the child. Decisions about access, however, will be based on what is best for the child (see page 27).

Travel overseas

Parents have the right to decide when their children travel abroad. In most cases this presents no difficulties. Difficulties can arise, however, if one parent threatens to take a child out of the country against the other parent's wishes. Where a court has awarded one parent custody, it will also usually say that the child must not be taken abroad without the court's permission or the written consent of both parents. Court proceedings can be taken to stop a child going abroad.

Parents can arrange their child's emigration but not where the court has made a custody order. In such a case the other parent's permission or the court's authority will need to be obtained.

Finance, property and the duty to maintain the child

Parents have the duty to maintain a child. This can extend to the father of an illegitimate child (see page 37).

If parents separate, neither lose the duty to maintain the child even if the child is not living with them. They can be ordered by the court to make payments to the child. The same applies if the child is in the care of the local authority—parents can be ordered to pay a contribution towards the child's upkeep. If the child is living with a parent who is claiming supplementary benefit, the other parent can be made to pay for the child under what is known as the Liable Relative Rule. Many of these obligations extend also to a step-parent who has assumed responsibility for the child.

Children who have reached the age of 16 can apply for an order for maintenance from their parents in matrimonial proceedings or custody proceedings. In some cases the child can apply up to the age of 21 years old. A younger child may be able to apply through the Official Solicitor if he has been appointed the child's *Guardian ad litem* (see page 12). Such applications are rare, partly because most parents do make proper arrangements for maintenance but also because most people are unaware that a child can apply in certain circumstances.

A child's property is his own and parents have no claim to it. They do have the power to administer a child's property but must do so carefully and honestly. It is not clear whether parents can charge a child under the age of 16 for accommodation should the child have sufficient property or income to be able to pay. If a child under the age of 18 dies, his or her parent would normally inherit the property unless a will existed that stated otherwise. If the child was married his or her spouse would inherit the property in the absence of any will.

Guardian

Parents have the right to appoint a guardian to look after the child on their death. This can be done either by deed or by will. Parents retain this right even if they do not have legal custody of the child. They can also appoint a guardian if the child is in the care of a local authority.

Marriage

Children under 16 cannot legally marry. Between the age of 16 and 18 a child needs the written consent of his or her parents before getting married. A child who manages to get married without proper parental consent is legally married but can be prosecuted.

The following conditions apply:

- A legitimate child with two parents living together will need the consent of both parents before getting married.

- If one parent has died, the consent of the surviving parent and any guardian who has been appointed is required.

- Where parents are divorced or separated the parent to whom custody has been granted can consent.

- A parent who has been deserted by the other parent can consent alone.

- If neither parent has custody the person who has custody needs to consent.

- If parents cannot be found to consent or are inaccessible the Registrar General of Births, Deaths and Marriages can consent.

Special circumstances operate when a child is in the care of a local authority (see page 74). The mother of an illegitimate child can give sole consent unless she has been deprived of custody by the court.

If consent is not forthcoming the child can apply to the High Court, county court or magistrates' court for permission to marry. A parent who actively opposes a child's wish to marry could make the child a ward of court. This prevents the child marrying without the court's permission. Most parental authority over a child ceases when a child gets married.

Adoption

Adoption orders cannot be made unless the child's parents consent or the court dispenses with the parent's consent. This applies to orders freeing the child for adoption as well.

In this context 'parents' means both parents of a legitimate child. In the case of an illegitimate child, only the mother's consent is required, unless the father has obtained a custody order in respect of the child, in which case both the mother and the father have to consent. The right to consent or withhold consent to adoption remains even if the child is in local authority care and cannot be taken away by any order of the court.

Parental arrangements for children under five

Child care at home

The law does not lay down any requirements for parents who wish to have their child looked after by someone else, for example, by a nanny, relative, friend or au pair.

However, anybody looking after a child can be prosecuted if they neglect a child. If a child is neglected he or she can be taken into care (see page 56).

Childminding

Many parents have their children looked after by childminders so that they can go out to work. The law imposes some controls on childminders who must be registered with the local authority's social services department if:

● they receive a child under the age of five into their home for more than two hours a day or for a longer period of up to six days;

● for payment, and where they are not a relative of the child.

Local authorities can impose a condition about the number of children who can be looked after by the childminder. They can also refuse to register a childminder.

The local authority can enter a childminder's home to inspect it and to observe the children looked after there, but it has no duty to supervise the childminder.

Nurseries

Nurseries have to be registered with the local authority if:

- they are situated in accommodation which is not used mainly as a private home; and

- where children under the age of 16 are looked after for more than two hours a day or for a longer period of up to six days.

This requirement operates regardless of whether or not the nursery demands or accepts any payment for looking after the children.

Local authorities can refuse to register nurseries or can impose conditions such as the number of staff to be employed, the standards of safety on the premises, feeding arrangements, keeping records and so on.

As with childminders, a person authorized by the local authority can enter a nursery to inspect the premises, the children and the arrangements made for their welfare.

Fostering

There are two types of foster parents. There are those who are paid by the local authority and who frequently look after children in local authority care. For more about local authority foster parents see page 67.

The other kind of foster parents are those who look after a person's child under a private arrangement made between the foster parents and the natural parent.

The law does impose some controls over private fostering arrangements. A foster parent has to notify the local authority social services department at least two, but not more than four, weeks before a child is placed with the foster parent. If a child is placed with a foster parent in an emergency the foster parent must notify the local authority within 48 hours.

The local authority can prohibit a private fostering arrangement or impose conditions on the foster parents such as the number of children the foster parent can look after or the fire precautions to be taken by the foster parent. Some people are by law disqualified from being foster parents. These include people convicted of certain criminal offences or those who have been refused registration as childminders.

The local authority has to visit all foster children in its area from time to time and can give advice on the care of foster children. It can inspect the foster parent's home and can, if it thinks that the arrangements are unsatisfactory, remove the child from the foster home by taking a place of safety order (see page 53).

For the purposes of the law a foster child is somebody who is under 16 when he or she went to live in the foster home and who remains there for more than six days. The law excludes from that definition the sorts of arrangements which are often made for friends to look after a child while parents are on holiday.

Foster parents do not acquire any of the parents' legal rights over the child, and if the parents request their child's return the foster parent must usually comply with this. However, foster parents can sometimes take wardship proceedings and can in certain circumstances apply for a custodianship order (see page 77) or to adopt the child (see page 44) and these may prevent parents resuming care of their child. Likewise, if the local authority takes proceedings (see page 56) this too could prevent parents from taking over the care of their child.

Custody

Most children grow up in the care of their parents and live in a home chosen by them. The children of married parents are deemed by law to be in the joint custody of each parent. The mother of an illegitimate child has sole custody of her child. In both cases, however, and particularly if parents separate or divorce the court can make a number of orders regulating the parents' rights.

Sole custody

When a court grants custody to one parent alone, it is usually called sole custody. Such an order means that the parent has the right to make the major decisions regarding the child's life, where the child lives and goes to school.

Increasingly, courts expect parents to consult each other on major decisions concerning their children, even where one parent has sole custody. If the court has made an order granting one parent sole custody that does not entitle that parent to take the child out of England or Wales without the consent of the other parent or the court.

Joint custody

Nowadays, courts frequently make joint custody orders. But while both parents share custody, care and control of the child is usually granted to the parent who is actually looking after the child. In such cases, parents are expected to make the big decisions about the child's life together. For this reason a joint custody order is often not appropriate if parents get on very badly. Not all courts are able to make joint custody orders (see page 31).

Care and control

An order for care and control gives the responsibility for providing for the child's day-to-day care to one parent. This parent will be solely responsible for routine matters such as making sure the child goes to school, is properly dressed and is adequately fed.

Legal custody

Some courts cannot make orders for joint custody but instead can award one parent legal custody. Where the court does this, it can also order that the person who is not given legal custody can retain all or such parental rights as the court specifies.

Access

The law takes the view that, save in very exceptional circumstances, all children have a right to access to their parents. This is often said to be a right of the child and not of the parents. Courts do not like refusing access to a parent and will only do so if, for example, that parent has badly ill-treated the child, or if access upsets the child. Courts tend to be sceptical of a parent who says that access upsets the child and may feel that it is really the parent who is upset or who is causing the child to be upset.

If parents can agree access terms between themselves the court normally just makes an order for 'reasonable access'. This leaves the child's parents to work out the detailed arrangements.

Courts can also order 'staying access'. This means that the child should be allowed to stay overnight or for longer periods with the parent who does not have custody of the child.

If parents cannot agree access arrangements the court may specify them in detail and make an order stating where, when and for what length of time access is to take place. Such an order is often called 'defined access'.

Disputes about custody

Custody disputes are very common when parents separate. Disputes about access are probably even more common.

In general, it is much better for the parents to try to reach agreement about custody. Parents can often be helped in this by conciliation services. These agencies exist to assist separating parents sort out financial as well as custody matters in an amicable way.

They are usually staffed by trained people and are run by social workers, the probation service, or specialized organizations, or organized by the courts. They are often free but sometimes a small charge is made if parents can afford to pay it. When asked to help with disputes about children many conciliation services will wish to see the children and discuss the matter with them. If agreement is not possible then parents have the right to apply to the court. There are a number of different procedures, depending on whether the parents are married or not, and, if they are, whether or not they are getting divorced.

Divorce and judicial separation proceedings

Whenever a married couple apply to the court for a decree of divorce or a decree of judicial separation they must file a document known as a 'petition'. Among other things this has to give the names and dates of birth of any children under 18 who are 'children of the family'. This includes not simply children born to both parents but also children born to one or other of the parents who have been part of the household. It does not include foster children, but does include adopted children.

If there are children then the person making the application must also complete a document known as the 'statement of arrangements for the children'. This is a standard form which asks for information about the children's home, education, health, maintenance, proposals for access and whether or not the child is in the care or under the supervision of a local authority.

Before a decree of divorce or judicial separation is made the court will want to see the parents or at least the parent who is looking after the children to discuss the arrangements. The court has to be satisfied that these are adequate, or the best that can be worked out in the circumstances. If the court is not satisfied it can order a Court Welfare Officer to prepare a report before making any orders concerning the children. If it thinks that there are circumstances which make it unsuitable or undesirable for the child to live with either of its parents, it can place the child in the care of the local authority. If it thinks that the supervision of the local authority is necessary it can make an order placing the child under the supervision of a social worker.

The court will not normally want to see the child but can make an order making the child a party to the proceedings. In this case the Official Solicitor will usually be appointed to represent the child (see page 12). Such orders are very rare.

If parents have reached agreement about custody and access the court is unlikely to interfere if it is satisfied that the children are being properly looked after. It will then make an order giving effect to the parents' agreement. If the parents have agreed that they should both have joint custody, with one parent having care and control and the other reasonable access, the court will simply make an order stating those terms.

In some courts, in particular the Divorce Registry in London, the parties may be asked to reach agreement about custody or access before the dispute is heard. The court will fix what is called a 'conciliation appointment' and will expect both parents and all the children over a certain age to come to the court and discuss the difficulties that have arisen with the Court Welfare Officer and a Registrar. This meeting is confidential and nothing that is said during the course of it can be used in subsequent proceedings. There have been considerable criticisms of this process particularly as it involves people trying to reach agreement on difficult issues in the confines of court buildings. However, it is one of the few procedures which enable children to express their views.

ORDERS FOR CUSTODY OR ACCESS

If parents cannot agree, either one can apply to the court in divorce or separation proceedings for an order for custody or access.

A form is available from the court for this application. The court will usually require sworn written statements from the parents and any witnesses that they wish to call. These are called 'affidavits'.

The case will be heard by a judge who will read the affidavits and listen to the parents and their witnesses. The court can order that a Court Welfare Officer's report be prepared before the case is decided.

Custody orders can always be overturned although this is unusual unless circumstances change. For example, if when the child is older, he or she wishes to live with the other parent, custody may be reconsidered.

Separation proceedings in the magistrates' court

Husbands and wives who separate can take proceedings in the magistrates' court without starting divorce or judicial separation proceedings. The magistrates' court can make orders for a child's maintenance and can also decide on custody disputes.

Evidence in the magistrates' court is given orally. The court can also ask a Court Welfare Officer to investigate the case and make a report.

The magistrates' court cannot make orders for joint custody but can make orders giving one parent legal custody and lay down what rights the other parent has. The magistrates' court can make orders for access.

Where proceedings have been started in the magistrates' court grandparents can apply for access.

If the court thinks there are circumstances which make it impracticable or undesirable for the child to live with either parent it can make a care order committing the child to the care of a local authority. It can also order that the child should be supervised by the local authority.

Other custody proceedings

A parent can apply to the magistrates' court, the county court or the High Court for a custody order without initiating divorce or separation proceedings. The choice of court is up to the person making the application, but normally the High Court would only be used if there was a particular difficulty. Magistrates' courts are probably not the best courts to use if the case is complicated but they may be quicker.

In these proceedings the court cannot make an order giving both parents joint custody but can give one parent legal custody and order that the other parent have such parental rights as it thinks proper. The court can also make an order for the non-custodial parent to have access. If it thinks there are circumstances making it impracticable or undesirable for the child to live with either of its parents it can make an order committing the child to the care of the local authority. It can also make a supervision order.

The procedure in the magistrates' court is the same as that for separation proceedings. In county courts and the High Court affidavits must be produced and the procedure is the same as that for divorce.

WARDSHIP PROCEEDINGS

Parents can also use wardship proceedings to resolve disputes about their children (see page 74).

Unmarried parents

The law does not give unmarried parents of children equal rights over their child. In law the mother of an illegitimate child has sole custody of the child. This is not a responsibility which she can agree to give away. However, the court can intervene and deprive the mother of custody.

The mother or father of an illegitimate child can apply to the magistrates' court, the county court or the High Court for a custody or access order. The choice of court is up to the person making the application and the procedure is exactly the same as that described on page 30. They can also apply to the court in wardship proceedings.

Child snatching

In recent years child snatching or kidnapping has become more common and the numbers of those children who are taken abroad has risen.

Recently the law regarding child snatching has been strengthened. It has always been a criminal offence to kidnap a child when the child is too young to be able to give proper agreement. It is also an offence for anyone acting without lawful authority or excuse to take a girl under the age of 16 out of the care of her parents, or those who look after her, without their permission (see page 159).

Many children are snatched by one of their parents, but until recently a parent whose child has been snatched by the other parent has not usually been able to rely on the criminal law or the police to assist. However, the law has now been changed so that anybody who abducts a child under 16, without lawful authority, from the care of the person entitled to the child's care commits an offence. This would include the removal of a child by a parent where the other parent had custody.

A person will not be guilty of the offence however if they can show that they believed the child was over 16, or, in the case of an illegitimate child, that that person had reasonable grounds for believing himself to be the father.

Police can arrest without a warrant a person who abducts a child in these circumstances. It ought now to be possible to obtain speedy police action.

It is also possible for an application to be made to the court for an order requiring the child to be returned.

If the parents are separated or divorced then the parent from whom the child has been taken can apply to the court for an order for the child to be returned. This applies where there is a custody order and the parents are not divorced.

If there are no proceedings then wardship proceedings can be started and an application made to the wardship court for an order that the child be returned (see page 76).

If the person who was looking after the child is afraid that the child will be taken abroad, an order should be obtained immediately from the court. If this is done the court should be told that the child might be taken abroad and then arrangements can be made for the Home Office to be notified to keep a watch on ports and airports. Applications to the court can in cases of very great urgency be made at weekends and out of office hours.

If a child is taken out of the country, the English courts have, at present, no power to order that a child be removed from a foreign country. The parent would have to take action in that foreign country in order to retrieve the child. This is complicated and expensive and the laws of some countries are phrased so that an order may not be made anyway. The Foreign and Commonwealth Office Consular Department can give advice and help although it cannot force a foreign government to return a child any more than the courts can.

There will soon be a new law which will enable the United Kingdom to sign two international conventions relating to the return of children who have been wrongfully removed. It will also mean that the courts of the United Kingdom and other countries which are signatories to the convention will recognize each other's custody decision. When this rule comes into force it should enable children to be returned from some foreign countries more easily. However, it has to be remembered that many foreign countries are not signatories to the convention.

Where a child abduction is feared, prevention is always better than cure and parents should be vigilant about their child's whereabouts. Schools can be alerted so as to prevent any unauthorized person taking the child home from school.

Maintenance for children

Legitimate children

The parents of a legitimate child both have a duty to maintain the child. When parents separate both parents continue to have this obligation regardless of whether they are looking after the child or not. Maintenance normally ends when the child becomes an adult or leaves school or full-time education.

BY AGREEMENT

Voluntary maintenance payments for children can be arranged without court proceedings. These are not enforceable if the parent stops paying them.

If agreed maintenance payments are incorporated into a deed they will always be treated as the wife's income and she will be liable to pay tax on them. Under a court order, however, payments can be made to the child and treated as the child's income. This can result in considerable tax savings. There is a quick and easy procedure for making agreements into maintenance orders in the magistrates' court.

BY COURT ORDER

If there are no divorce proceedings, an application for a maintenance order can be made in the magistrates' court. This can formalize an agreement between husband and wife. Otherwise, either parent can apply in the magistrates' court, county court or High Court for a custody order. If the parents are married the court can then make an order for maintenance.

The mechanics of applying vary according to which court is used. In the magistrates' court the procedure is very much the same as that mentioned previously. If the application is made in the county court or High Court affidavits will have to be prepared.

If there are divorce or judicial separation proceedings, maintenance for children can be applied for at any time after the proceedings have started.

Maintenance orders usually last until the child is 16 or 17 but can be extended until the child finishes full-time education or training, usually until the child is 18. In special cases, for example, where the child is ill, they can continue for longer.

HOW MAINTENANCE IS CALCULATED

There is no formula used by the courts to work out how much maintenance should be paid for children. The amounts vary widely. Magistrates' courts tend to make lower orders than the divorce courts.

When calculating how much to order, the court should take into account:

- the income of the husband and the wife and what it costs them to earn it

- the needs of the children and how much it costs to keep them

- the needs and expenses of the husband and wife

- the tax and benefit implications

The court should put the needs of the children first. Wherever possible, the court will try to make an order so that the child can be brought up in the same way and to the same standard as if the couple still lived together.

These considerations do not always help the courts to decide. People often don't realize just how much it costs to keep a child. It is often useful for a parent to keep a note of everything spent on a child over several weeks before the hearing. By the time every bus fare and packet of sweets is taken into account the figures can be very surprising.

Courts sometimes use the DHSS allowances for calculating supplementary benefit as a guide for working out maintenance payments for children. At present these are:

- £10.10 per week for each child under 11

- £15.10 per week for each child aged 11 to 15

- £18.20 per week for each child aged 16 or 17

These allowances are increased every year.

An alternative guide is the rate recommended by the National Foster Care Association as suitable pay for foster parents. At present it is:

- £22.55 per week for a child aged between 0 and 4

- £29.75 per week for a child aged between 5 and 7

- £32.62 per week for a child aged between 8 and 10

- £35.42 per week for a child aged between 11 and 12

- £38.29 per week for a child aged between 13 and 15

- £51.03 per week for a child aged between 16 and 18

An increase of 14 percent is payable for children living in London.
Since foster parents are not entitled to child benefit, if these
guidelines are followed strictly, child benefit should be deducted
(at present £7.00 per week, plus a single-parent addition of £4.55
per week).

LUMP SUM PAYMENTS

In divorce proceedings the court can order that a lump sum of
money be paid to or for the child. In separation proceedings in
the magistrates' court lump sum payments) can also be ordered
up to £500 per child.

SCHOOL FEES

None of these figures take into account fees for private education.
Most school fees are very high and dramatically alter the level of
child maintenance needed. They also increase regularly, a problem
that can be overcome by obtaining a 'school fees order' which
provides that the parent should pay the child's school fees and at
a rate that varies automatically when the fees increase. Difficulties
can arise if the order is not expressed properly, and legal advice
should be sought.

VARYING MAINTENANCE ORDERS

All maintenance orders can be altered by making an application
to the court. There is no provision for making a maintenance
order which varies according to the rate of inflation, although some
courts now do make orders which provide that the maintenance
will be adjusted each year in accordance with changes in the retail
price index. This avoids the need to make another application to
the court.

Illegitimate children

BY AGREEMENT

Where the parents of an illegitimate child are living with each
other they will usually both contribute to the upkeep of the child.
If they live apart then there is nothing to stop them agreeing
arrangements for maintenance.The person who pays the
maintenance will not get tax relief on the payments unless a deed
is drawn up. If this is done the payments made will be treated as
the mother's income and she will have to pay tax on them if her
income is over the level of the personal allowance. For this

reason it is better to get a court order for maintenance so that the payments can be treated as the child's income.

BY COURT ORDER

There is only one way in which the mother of an illegitimate child can obtain a maintenance order and that is through affiliation proceedings in the magistrates' court. This is worth doing if the father either refuses to pay or pays only occasionally. Only the mother can apply for an affiliation order. The father has no such right.

She must make the application either before the baby is born or within three years of the birth, unless the father has already contributed to the child's upbringing in which case she can make the application within three years of the last contribution he made. If the mother applies to the court before the baby is born the application will not be heard by the court until after the birth.

The mother must be a 'single woman' when she applies. If she is married she will still be counted as single if she is not in a position to be supported by her husband. This definition has been held to include a woman who is separated from her husband at the time she has the child.

When the case is heard the court first has to decide that the man alleged to be the father is the father. Only after it has done that can it make an order for maintenance.

Where there is no dispute about who is the father this will not present a problem. Where there is, the court will have to hear evidence. The woman's evidence alone is not enough and must be corroborated by other facts. Previous statements by the man that he is the father, as shown on the child's birth certificate, for example, or evidence from other people that the man and woman had the necessary relationship can provide the proof that is needed.

Sometimes where there is a dispute the court will order blood tests to be done. The man and the child will both be required to have blood samples taken. These are then analysed. Comparison of the two blood samples can show whether or not the man could be the father. They cannot show that he definitely is the father, but whether it is likely that he is. Although the court can order blood tests it cannot force the man to comply by giving a sample of blood.

If the court finds that the man is the father it can then go on to make a maintenance order. When doing so the court should consider the needs of the child and its income, if any, as well as the needs, income and earning capacity of both the mother and the father. The level of maintenance orders made by magistrates' courts in affiliation cases is notoriously low and this, together with the potentially embarrassing nature of the case itself, probably explains why very few women apply.

The court can make several types of order.

TYPES OF ORDER

The court can order that the father pay maintenance, either 'for' the child or 'to' the child. If the order is payable 'to' the child it will be treated as the child's income by the Inland Revenue and so will not be taxable unless the total income exceeds the child's personal allowance for income tax. If the order is payable 'for' the child it will be treated as the mother's income for tax purposes.

If the application was made before the child was born or within two months of the birth the order can be backdated to that date. Otherwise it can only be backdated to the date on which the application was made.

The maintenance order will last until the child is 16 although it can be varied or cancelled during that time. If the child continues in education or training after 16, the order can be continued until 18, or even longer if the child continues in education or training. The father's obligation to pay does not end if the mother marries, only if the child is adopted, say by the mother or her new husband.

For ways of calculating the level of child maintenance see page 34. In theory, at least, the way in which maintenance is worked out should be the same whether the child is legitimate or not.

Apart from maintenance orders, the court can order that the father pay a lump sum of up to £500. It can also order that he pay a lump sum to cover the expenses of the birth. This includes the costs of the layette, such as clothes, nappies, pram, bedding. If the child has died before the order is made the court can also order the father to pay the funeral expenses.

Enforcing maintenance orders

Maintenance orders are often not paid. As most orders are payable by fathers this section is written as though it is the father who has defaulted.

Enforcing a maintenance order can be difficult, particularly if the father is unemployed or self-employed. The most effective ways to enforce maintenance orders are described here.

THROUGH THE MAGISTRATES' COURT

If the maintenance order was made in the magistrates' court, the magistrates' court can enforce it. If the maintenance order was made in the divorce court, the divorce court can order that the maintenance be registered in the magistrates' court so it can be enforced there. It is usually quicker and easier to enforce the order through a magistrates' court than through a divorce court.

If the father does not pay, the mother can go to the magistrates' court and can apply for a summons. This means that the father will have to appear in court and explain why he hasn't paid. If he still does not pay he can be sent to prison, but this solution rarely does anybody any good and can cause tremendous bitterness.

'ATTACHMENT OF EARNINGS ORDER'

If the father is in regular employment an 'attachment of earnings order' is perhaps the best way of ensuring that maintenance is paid. This order can be made in a divorce or magistrates' court and means that the maintenance will be deducted from the man's wages by his employer. The employer will send the maintenance to the court, who will then send it on to the woman. The order can include an amount to pay off any arrears.

Attachment of earnings orders cannot be made where the man is self-employed or unemployed.

OTHER METHODS

In rare cases the father's goods can be seized and sold, or any money in a bank account used to pay maintenance.

Illegitimate Children

The law relating to illegitimate children developed in an era when illegitimacy was seen as a social stigma, the result of a liaison between a promiscuous mother and irresponsible father. Times have changed. Many children who are born to unmarried parents today are born as the result of long-term unions which are often just as stable, if not more so than many marriages. Their parents have often chosen not to get married, a trend that is on the increase. In 1984 slightly over one in every six children were illegitimate.

The law has almost entirely failed to take account of these social changes. As a result illegitimate children today suffer some legal disadvantages from their status although the social stigma has all but disappeared.

Who is illegitimate?

An illegitimate child is one whose parents were unmarried either at the time the child was conceived or at the time the child was born. Parents who married after the child was conceived but before the child was born will have a legitimate child.

If the parents' marriage is void, because one of the parents was under 16 at the time they got married, for example, then the child will be illegitimate. If the marriage is valid although entered into illegally, because a parent was between 16 and 18 and had not obtained parental consent before getting married, for example, the child would probably be legitimate.

If the marriage was invalid but at the time of the marriage, or when the child was conceived, either or both of the parents believed that the marriage was valid, the child will be legitimate as long as the father was living in England and Wales at the date of the child's birth.

Where parents are married the law presumes that the child is legitimate but this can always be challenged in the courts. If at the time of the child's birth the parents were legally separated the law presumes that the child is illegitimate.

Legitimization

A child becomes legitimate when his or her parents get married. The child's parents should then re-register the birth. Once this is done, the child has virtually all the rights of a legitimate child although there can be some consequences for inheritance rights.

Consequences of illegitimacy

Illegitimacy has consequences both for the child and for the parents. The most significant and far-reaching consequences are those which affect the child's father.

Parental rights

The mother has sole parental rights and duties if the child is illegitimate. This means that she has a right to choose the child's name, the right to bring up the child and the other parental rights and duties set out in Chapter 2.

One of the most serious consequences for a father is that the mother alone has the power to consent to the child's adoption. Although the father of an illegitimate child can oppose adoption proceedings and apply for custody, his rights are much less than those of the mother.

Since the father of an illegitimate child is not treated as a parent in care cases and similar proceedings he will also not have the right to oppose the making of a care order or the making of a Parental Rights Resolution. However, his rights are much greater if the local authority brings wardship proceedings to obtain a care order since there are no restrictions on his participation.

Paternity

The child will only have evidence of his or her paternity if the father's name is on the birth certificate. This can be done only if both the mother and father agree to it or the mother has obtained an affiliation order (see page 37). The only other way in which paternity can legally be established under English law is if the mother successfully takes affiliation proceedings in the magistrates' court (see page 37).

Maintenance

The mother of an illegitimate child is severely limited in what she can do to apply for maintenance from the father. The only way open to her is through affiliation proceedings (see page 37).

Although both the mother and the father of an illegitimate child can apply for custody in custody proceedings (see page 31) or for orders in wardship proceedings, the court cannot make maintenance orders. This does not mean parents cannot agree to make payments themselves (see page 36).

Nationality

The consequences for a child whose parents are not married can be serious. British nationality law provides that a child takes his nationality and citizenship from the nationality of his parents. In the case of an illegitimate child this means the mother alone. Undoubtedly some children lose the right to British citizenship because of this (see Chapter 11).

Inheritance

The law here is much more favourable to illegitimate children than might be supposed. A man has always been able to leave property in his will to a named illegitimate child. In the past if he left property to his child this was presumed to exclude any illegitimate children unless specifically stated. Nor was it possible to leave property to an unborn child.

The law has now been changed and gifts in wills to children include illegitimate children. This extends to gifts to nephews, nieces and grandchildren.

In addition, the law which allows a child to claim from a parent's estate, if that parent dies without making a will, has been extended so that an illegitimate child can make a claim equally with any legitimate children. However, illegitimate children cannot claim against the estates of their grandparents, brothers or sisters, uncles and aunts who die without making wills, although legitimate children can.

Where a man makes a will but does not make reasonable provision for his children, both illegitimate and legitimate children can now make a claim.

Adoption

Adoption transfers the legal status and all the rights of the natural parents to the adoptive parents. Usually, but not always, the adoptive parents are not related to the child at all. Sometimes, however, children are adopted by one of their natural parents and a step-parent. This happens, for example, when the mother of an illegitimate child later marries and the couple wish to share responsibility for the child and have the same legal rights. Children can be adopted by relatives, but this is not common. Many children in the care of local authorities who are not returned to live with their parents are adopted by other people.

When children are adopted they receive new birth certificates which show the adopted parents as their parents but make it clear that this is due to adoption. An adoption order cannot be made if the child is over 18 or is or has been married.

The adoption process

All adoption orders must be made by a court. The legal process of adoption is very strictly controlled. Today a child can normally only be adopted through an adoption agency or society. These organizations make the arrangements for the child to be placed with new parents.

A child can be adopted without the intervention of an adoption agency in the following circumstances.

- if the child is to be adopted by a parent and step-parent

- if the adopter is a relative of the child. This means grandparent, brother, sister, uncle or aunt, and, if the child is illegitimate, the child's father

- if the High Court has authorized an adoption application (see page 77)

- if the child who is being adopted is from overseas.

- if the adopters are the child's foster parent. This is complicated though, and legal advice should be sought.

Adoption agencies and societies

There are two types of adoption agencies and societies—voluntary bodies often set up by church organizations, and local authorities acting as adoption agencies. All adoption agencies have to be approved by the Department of Health and Social Security and have to comply with regulations. These controls are designed to ensure that the decisions they make are the result of proper investigation and that the child's interests are protected. Adoption agencies investigate both the children who are to be placed for adoption and the adoptive parents.

Children placed for adoption

Each agency must set up a panel consisting of at least some of the agency's employees and including a medical advisor. The agency must also take legal advice for some of its decisions.

Before a child can be placed for adoption the agency must make detailed inquiries about the child and his or her parents, and obtain medical reports about the child's health. Adoption agencies investigate thoroughly any child they are considering placing for adoption.

The adoption agency will then assess the information that they have and decide whether or not the child's best interests will be met by an adoption order. They must also consider whether or not it would be better for the child to be freed for adoption (see page 000). A child cannot be placed for adoption until these decisions have been made.

Adoptive parents

Adoption agencies also investigate the circumstances and history of anyone who applies to be considered as an adoptive parent.

Most adoptions are by married couples. The agency will obtain medical reports, take up references from two friends of the adopters, study their personal and financial circumstances, find out about their home and look at their reasons for wishing to adopt. These investigations are intended to determine whether or not the candidates are suitable people to adopt a child. Until they are approved by the agency, a child cannot be placed with them for adoption.

Approval is not always unconditional. The agency may consider the couple suitable adopters for one child, say a young baby, but not for an older child.

As there are more people wishing to adopt children than children waiting to be adopted, approval does not mean that the couple will immediately be given a child. They will be kept on the adoption agency's list until a suitable child becomes available. The British Agencies for Adoption and Fostering (BAAF) and Parent to Parent Information Adoption Service (PPIAS) have arrangements to enable adopters to find out about children available for adoption in other areas.

Placing the child with adopters

Once the agency has decided to place a child for adoption it must then try to find suitable parents. If suitable adopters are not available on the agency's own list, then the agency will usually make inquiries from the Adoption Resource Exchange, organized by the British Agencies for Adoption and Fostering, or it may advertise in the press. If people come forward who are not already approved for adoption they will have to be investigated and approved before the child can be placed with them.

Once the agency has found suitable adopters it must review the child's position again and the circumstances of the adopters and decide whether or not the adopters are suitable for that particular child. Once that decision has been made, the child can be placed with the adopters for adoption. The child can go and live with the adopters before that decision is made but they will not be able to apply to the court to adopt until the agency has decided that the child can be placed with them for adoption.

Applying for an adoption order

All adoption orders must be made by the court. The application can be made to either the High Court, county court or magistrates' court. Normally magistrates' courts only deal with simple, straightforward cases. If the child is a ward of court then the application to adopt must be made in the High Court. The High Court's permission has to be obtained before the application can be made.

The application is made by the people wishing to adopt the child. A married couple must make the application jointly. If a married person applies alone then the court must be satisfied that the husband or wife cannot be found or that the couple are living apart and separation is permanent, or that the other partner to the marriage is, through ill-health, incapable of making an application for an adoption order. Single, widowed or divorced people can also apply. All those applying for adoption must be over 21 years old. Before an adoption order can be made the child must have lived with the adopters for 13 weeks. In some cases this is extended to 12 months.

The adoption application is made on a form. The applicants must give the following information:

● name, address, occupation and date of birth

● relationship if any to the child

● the name, sex and date of birth of the child

● the names of the child's parents and their addresses

● details of who has legal custody or care of the child and who, if anybody, is liable to maintain the child

● what names the adopters propose that the child should have if adopted

● details of how long the child has lived with the adopters, and, if the child was placed for adoption by an agency, the date on which the child was placed for adoption

● details of any court proceedings that have taken place in relation to the child

● the child's nationality

If the child was not placed with the adopters by an adoption agency the applicants must also provide medical reports on their health as well as the child's health, and the names of two referees and give three months' notice to the local authority. Where a natural parent and a step-parent are applying to adopt, medical reports and references are not necessary. All adopters have to send the court a copy of their marriage certificate if they are married and a copy of the child's birth certificate.

An adoption order can only be made with the consent of both the child's natural parents if they were married, or the child's mother if the child is illegitimate. The application form must therefore state whether the child's parent or parents consent to the adoption. If they do not, the adopters must supply a statement of facts which sets out the reasons why they ask the court to dispense with the parents' consent.

In country courts and the High Court a fee is payable when an adoption application is issued, currently £55 in the High Court and £25 is in the county court. No fee is payable in the magistrates' court.

Confidentiality

Many people applying for an adoption order do not wish the natural parents of the child to know their identity or address. They should then ask the court for a confidential serial number. This means that the natural parents will not be sent any of the adoption forms except the statement of facts.

After the application is made

Within six weeks of the application being issued the adoption agency who has authorized the placement must file a report which provides considerable detail about the child, the natural parents and the adopters, and the procedure that the adoption agency has gone through before making the placement. The agency should also give its opinion about the appropriateness of making an adoption order. This report is often called a 'Schedule 2 Report'.

Guardians ad litem *and Reporting Officers*

The court must then appoint a *Guardian ad litem* or Reporting Officer. They are appointed from panels.

A Reporting Officer will be appointed if the parents agree to an adoption order being made. In such a case, the Reporting Officer will check that the parents' agreement is given freely and that they understand what is involved. The Reporting Officer also witnesses the parents' signatures to a formal document in which they give their consent. Parents can withdraw their consent at any time before an adoption order is made.

A *Guardian ad litem* will be appointed either where one or both of the parents does not consent, or the court feels that there are special circumstances which make such an appointment necessary. A *Guardian ad litem*'s job is to investigate all the circumstances surrounding the adoption. The Guardian must also advise the court whether the child should be present at the hearing of the adoption application. The court may also ask the *Guardian ad litem* to investigate other aspects of the case that it feels are relevant. In adoption cases in the High Court the *Guardian ad litem* is normally the Official Solicitor. The *Guardian ad litem* will prepare a report setting out the results of the investigation. In adoption cases this can only be disclosed with the court's permission.

The adoption hearing

Adoption hearings take place in private. The only people who will be allowed into the court are the parties to the case and others directly concerned with it, such as the adoption agency's representative.

In the High Court and county court the case will be heard by a judge. In the magistrates' court it will be heard by magistrates.

The applicants and the child's parents can be represented by lawyers. Legal aid is available for such cases. Children are represented in adoption cases by their *Guardian ad litem*.

Dispensing with parental consent

If the natural parents do not consent to the adoption, their consent can be dispensed with if one of the following circumstances apply:

● the parent cannot be found or is incapable of giving agreement

- the parent is withholding agreement unreasonably
- the parent has persistently failed without reasonable cause to discharge the parental duties in relation to the child
- the parent has abandoned or neglected the child
- the parent has persistently ill-treated the child
- the parent has seriously ill-treated the child and it is unlikely that the child will go back to live in the parent's home

The consent of the father of an illegitimate child does not have to be given unless the father has obtained an order giving him custody of the child. He can still oppose the adoption on the grounds that it is not in the child's interests to be adopted.

The child's interests

The court also has to be satisfied that an adoption order is in the child's best interests, it must give consideration to the need to safeguard and promote the child's welfare throughout childhood. In addition the court must establish what the wishes and feelings of the child are and assess these in the light of the child's age and understanding. An older child's view can be of very great importance. Children are frequently seen by judges before adoption orders are made. They usually see the judge in his room for an informal chat.

Types of order in adoption cases

After reviewing all the evidence, the court may make an adoption order so that the adopters are now the child's legal parents. If, however, the court decides against this, there are other orders it can make:

- an interim adoption order. This can last two years and can only be made if the parents have already consented to the adoption or the court has dispensed with their consent (see above). Interim adoption orders are very rarely made. At the end of the time the court can make an adoption order.

- a care order, placing the child in the care of a local authority (see page 64). In such a case a court can order either or both natural parents to pay maintenance for the child. It can only make a court order if the child is under 16.

- a supervision order, placing the child under the supervision of an independent person, or local authority, or probation officer. It can only do this if the child is under 16.

- a custodianship order (see page 77). A court can make a custodianship order if it feels that, although the requirements for an adoption order are satisfied, it would be more appropriate to take this action. This order is likely to be made if the natural parents are still seeing the child.

- no order at all. In this case the child's legal status remains as it was before the adoption application was made. If a child was in the care of a local authority the child remains in care. If the child was informally placed with the applicants by the parents then the child remains in the legal custody of the parent.

Knowledge about natural parents

Adopted children have the right to see their original birth records when they reach 18. The information can also be made available to an adopted child under 18 who is planning to get married.

Records will reveal the identity of the child's natural parents and can help a child trace them. A counselling service is available for those wishing to see their birth records and is obligatory in the case of children adopted before 26 November 1976.

Application is made to the Registrar General for births, deaths and marriages.

Birth certificates

Adopted children receive a new birth certificate which gives their new names and the identity of their adoptive parents. A copy of one is illustrated on page 52.

52

Application No................

QHA 014201

CERTIFIED COPY OF AN ENTRY

1. No. of entry	
	Registration District
2. Date..	
and	....
	Sub-district
country of birth of child	....
3. Name and surname of child	
4. Sex of child	
5. Name and surname	
address	
and	
occupation of adopter or adopters	
6. Date of adoption order	
and description of court by which made	
7. Date of entry	
8. Signature of officer deputed by Registrar General to attest the entry	

SPECIMEN

CERTIFIED to be a true copy of an entry in the Adopted Children Register maintained at the GENERAL REGISTER OFFICE, Titchfield, Fareham, Hants. Given at the General Register Office, under the seal of the said Office.

on.. 19...........

This certificate is issued pursuant to the Adoption Act 1958.

By Section 20 of the Act, a certified copy of an entry in the Adopted Children Register, if purporting to be sealed or stamped with the seal of the General Register Office shall, without any further or other proof of the entry, be received as evidence of the adoption to which it relates.

Adoption certificate

Form A508A 8349845 2/85 1,500 Mcr. (306216)

Care

Although most children are brought up by their parents, a small, but significant number are looked after by local authorities. These children are said to be 'in care'. There are approximately 94,000 children in care in England and Wales. Proportionately more children are in care in urban than in rural areas. There are two main types of care: voluntary and compulsory.

Children can come into the care of the local authority in a variety of ways and can stay in care for different lengths of time. Many children go into care for very short periods at their parents' request, in order to help the family meet a domestic crisis, perhaps because one of the parents has to go into hospital.

Other children are in compulsory care and may remain in care for all their childhood. Increasingly, if a child is not going to be returned home the local authority will try to have the child adopted by another family.

Emergencies

Emergencies occur in many families and the law provides procedures to deal with these. If a family crisis occurs which makes it impossible for the parents to look after the child then the local authority can receive the child into voluntary care.

In other circumstances a 'place of safety' order may be appropriate. Other emergencies can be dealt with by applying to the court in wardship proceedings (see page 74).

'Place of safety' orders

A 'place of safety' order gives the holder the power to remove the child from home to a place of safety. A place of safety may be a children's home, hospital or any other place where the child will be protected. It is an emergency order and should only be granted if the child is in real danger or has suffered harm. There are three types of place of safety order.

The commonest is an order granted by a magistrate. This can remain in force for up to 28 days. It can be made if the magistrate is satisfied that any of the grounds for bringing care proceedings exist (except the offence condition) (see page 57). Place of safety orders can also be made to prevent child entertainers being sent abroad (see page 102). Anyone can apply for the order and there is no right of appeal against it or any right to apply to the court to have it discharged.

The second type of order authorizes the police to search for a child and take the child to a place of safety. Anyone can apply for this and the magistrates will grant it if they are satisfied that the child is being ill-treated or harmed. Apart from giving the police officer the power to search for the child this order also allows them to enter the child's home, using force if necessary.

In the third case, a police officer can detain a child in a place of safety for up to eight days without applying to a magistrate if he has reasonable cause to believe that any of the grounds for bringing care proceedings, except the offence condition, or the education condition, exist (see page 57). This does not give the police the power to enter premises to search for the child, but only to detain the child.

If a child is detained under these circumstances an officer not below the rank of Inspector should be told as soon as possible. He should investigate the circumstances and can release the child. If not, the child and parents can apply to the court for the child to be released. The court must order the child's release unless it thinks that would not be in the child's interests. Unfortunately legal aid is not available for such applications, although if there is a duty solicitor at the court he or she may be able to help.

Place of safety orders are often followed by care proceedings. Once they are granted the local authority will usually take over the child's care.

Voluntary care

Over half the children in care in England and Wales are in voluntary care. This means that no court has made an order forcing the parents to put their child into care. Most of these children stay in care for a short time and then return to live with their parents.

In certain circumstances a local authority has a duty to receive a child into care. It must do this where a child is lost, or has no parents or guardians, or has been abandoned by them, or where the child's parents or guardians are unable to look after the child, because they are ill for example. If one of these circumstances exists and the local authority feel that their intervention is necessary to protect the child's welfare, they must receive the child into voluntary care.

Although the local authority has a duty to keep the child in its care as long as the child's welfare requires it, it should also try to ensure that the care of the child is taken over by a parent, guardian, relative or friend, if that is in the child's interests.

The local authority cannot receive a child over 17 years old into care. A child can stay in voluntary care until he or she is 18 years old.

When a child is in voluntary care the local authority has to provide the child with a home. This will normally be a children's home if the stay in care is short. If a child is very young or is likely to stay in care for a longer period of time, then the local authority are more likely to place the child with foster parents.

Parents should be told where the child is living and allowed to visit. They also have the right to ask for their child to be returned to them. If, however, a child has been in voluntary care for more than six months, parents have to give the local authority 28 days' notice of their wish to have the child home. Such a notice must be given in writing. A simple letter is sufficient. If the local authority wants to return the child before the 28 days' notice is up they can do so. If they don't think it would be in the child's interests to go back to live with the parents at all then they have 28 days in which to take steps to take over the parents' rights. They could either make the child a ward of court (see page 74) or they could take a Parental Rights Resolution (see page 62).

Children in voluntary care for a very long time will probably have been placed with foster parents. If they have lived with those foster parents for more than three years, or one year if the parents consent, the foster parents can apply to the court for a custodianship order which, if granted, would mean that neither the local authority nor the child's parents could insist on the child's removal from the foster parents' home (see page 77). Alternatively, in some circumstances the foster parents could make the child a ward of court and ask the court to make an order preventing the child from returning to live with the parents.

Compulsory care

There are a number of ways in which a child can be taken into the care of a local authority against the parents' wishes. At present the government is undertaking a review of all these legal procedures and it is likely that they will change in the course of the next five years.

A child can be made the subject of a care order in the following ways:

- in care proceedings
- in custody, divorce, or adoption proceedings
- under a Parental Rights Resolution
- in wardship proceedings

Conditions for care

The local authority, or in some cases, the local education authority, the NSPCC or the police can apply to the juvenile court for a care order or a supervision order. (For more about the juvenile court see page 3.) If a care order is made the child will be placed in the care of the local authority.

Before the court can make a care or supervision order it first has to be satisfied that one of the conditions set out below exists. This is often known as the 'primary condition'. Secondly the court has to be satisfied that the child needs to be in care. This is known as the 'care and control test'.

The primary conditions

These are:

● that the child's proper development or that of a brother or sister is being impaired or neglected or the child or a brother or sister is being ill-treated or neglected, or that this is likely to happen because a person who has been convicted of an offence involving ill-treatment or neglect to children is, or may become, a member of the household to which the child belongs.

This covers most forms of ill-treatment to a child whether at the hands of a parent, step-parent or other family member. The ill-treatment does not have to be physical but can consist of mental cruelty. The court does not have to decide who caused the harm, it is enough that the child suffered harm which could have been prevented.

● that the child is exposed to moral danger. This is sometimes used where a child's mother or father is running a brothel or works as a prostitute. It can be used where older children come under the influence of undesirable adults or even other children.

● that the child is beyond parental control. This ground is often used where an older child refuses to live with his or her parents or runs away from home. It also covers situations where a parent cannot control the child.

● that the child is of compulsory school age but is not receiving suitable and efficient full-time education (see page 85).

● that the child has committed an offence other than homicide. This is usually called the offence condition and is very rarely used. If a child is thought to have committed an offence he or she will usually be prosecuted (see Chapter 14).

The care and control test

If the court finds that one or more of these conditions exists it still cannot make an order unless it is also satisfied that the child is in need of care and control which he or she will not receive unless an order is made.

Orders the court can make

Once the court is satisfied that the right conditions exist, it will go on to consider what, if any, order to make. It can make one of the following orders.

Supervision order

The most common order is a supervision order, placing the child under the supervision of the local authority for up to three years or until the child's eighteenth birthday, whichever is the sooner (see page 74).

Care order

The other common order is one that takes the child into care. The implications of that are discussed on page 64.

Recognizance

The court can also order that the parent or guardian enters into a 'recognizance', that is, a promise made to the court to take proper care of the child and exert proper control, on penalty of payment of a fixed sum of up to £1000 if this is not done. Parents have to agree to this. A recognizance can only last for up to three years or until the child is 18, whichever is sooner. Recognizances are very rarely ordered.

Hospital and guardianship orders

These orders can only be made where a child is suffering from a mental illness. A hospital order commits a child to hospital for treatment, whereas a guardianship order allows the child to be treated in the community and gives parental powers to the person appointed guardian—usually the local authority.

The court must have evidence from two doctors saying that the child is sufficiently ill to justify the making of the order and must also be satisfied that this is the most suitable way of dealing with the child.

Hospital and guardianship orders last for six months but can be renewed for six months and annually after that, without a court order. Complicated provisions exist for the discharging of these orders and legal advice should be sought. They are very rarely made.

Care proceedings

The procedure for taking a child into care is complicated and unusual. The case is normally initiated by the local authority, sometimes by the NSPCC or police. If the allegation is that the child is not receiving proper education then the case must be brought by the local education authority.

Care proceedings can be started by the local authority taking out a notice or a 'summons' which tells the child and the parents to appear before the court. If they do not come a warrant can be issued which will result in the child and/or the parents being arrested and brought before the court. Many care proceedings are effectively started by a place of safety order being made (see page 53).

If the child is under five-years-old the court can excuse the child's attendance. If the child is over five but cannot come to court because of illness or accident the court cannot make a care order, although it could make an interim care order.

Interim care orders

Often the court will not be able to hear the case when it first comes to court and will have to adjourn it. When it does so it may not make an order, in which case the child will continue to live with the parents. Otherwise, the court can make an interim care order. This lasts for up to 28 days and places the child in the care of the local authority for that time. The court is likely to make such an order if it thinks that the child might come to harm if left at home.

The court can only make a first interim care order if the child attends the court, or is under five years old or cannot be there because of illness or accident. The child, or the parents on the child's behalf, can apply to the juvenile court or the High Court to discharge an interim care order.

Separate representation orders

Technically all care proceedings are brought against the child and not the parents. The child's interests and the parents' interests are presumed to coincide.

Often, however, this will not be the case. If, for example, the child has been ill-treated by the parents then their interests cannot be said to be the same. Where it is thought that such a conflict of interest might exist the court should make a separate representation order and appoint a *Guardian ad litem* to represent the child. The *Guardian ad litem* may then instruct a solicitor to appear for the child in court. Legal aid is available for the child. A separate representation order does not mean that there is a conflict of interest between the child and the parents but just that that is a possibility. These orders are common.

If a separate representation order is not made then the parents can instruct a solicitor to act on behalf of the child. If a separate representation order is made, the parents are entitled to ask for a solicitor to represent them and apply for legal aid.

The Guardian ad litem

The *Guardian ad litem* has the job of preparing a report for the court. He or she will be chosen from a panel of senior and experienced social workers. They will not necessarily be employed by any local authority and must not be employed by the local authority who is bringing the case. They should be independent of the local authority and the parents.

The *Guardian ad litem* should investigate the case, look at the local authority's records and files and see everybody who is relevant including, of course, the child and the child's parents. The guardian will prepare a report to be shown to the court, stating an opinion about which order should be made.

The *Guardian ad litem* and the child's solicitor will usually work together. The child's solicitor should also see the child and interview any relevant witnesses. If a child is old enough to give the solicitor clear instructions then the solicitor must follow them even if he or she and the guardian disagree with them. If, as is often the case, the child is too young to do this then the solicitor for the child must take instructions from the guardian.

There has been some criticism of this practice. One of the difficulties is that it is not always easy to decide when a child is capable of giving instructions. Another difficulty is that the *Guardian ad litem* has an ambivalent role. In the case of a young child, the guardian is effectively representing the child. In the case of an older child, the guardian will not be representing the child but will instead be expressing a view as to what should happen which may well conflict with the child's wishes. Here it is important to remember that the solicitor must take instructions from the child and not the guardian.

The child's solicitor can call witnesses on behalf of the child, and the child can also give evidence. The parents can give evidence themselves and can also call witnesses to answer any allegations about them. Most courts allow parents the freedom to say what they wish.

Reports

If the court finds the primary condition and the care and control test proved it will then have to consider what order, if any, to make. At this stage the court will read any reports that have been prepared. These will include the *Guardian ad litem*'s report, if one has been appointed, and also any reports from the local authority and the child's school. Medical and psychiatric reports may also be prepared. Although reports give a detailed account of the child and the family, it is not unusual for them to be inaccurate in some respects.

The child and parents can see the reports but are not entitled to. If they don't, the magistrates must either read the reports aloud or inform them about anything in the reports which influences them in deciding what order to make. The magistrates can adjourn the case for extra reports to be prepared.

Revoking the order

If a care order is made it will not be for a fixed period of time and the child or the parents can apply to revoke the care order. This application can be made every six months. The same applies to supervision orders.

Appeals

If a care, supervision, hospital or guardianship order is made, the child can appeal against it to the crown court where the case will be reheard. The local authority cannot appeal if it loses the case. It can, however, make the child a ward of court. This will mean that the case is reheard.

Care and supervision orders in other proceedings

In divorce and custody proceedings (see Chapter 2), in wardship proceedings (see page 74), and in adoption proceedings (see Chapter 4) the court has the power to make a care order if it thinks it is undesirable or impracticable for the child to live with either of its parents. The court can also make a supervision order in such proceedings, if it seems desirable to do so.

Parental Rights Resolutions

Parental Rights Resolutions deprive parents of their rights over the child. The effect is mostly the same as that of a care order (see page 64).

A Parental Rights Resolution is not made by the court but by the local authority's social services committee. They can take this action if the child is in voluntary care *and* one of the following conditions is satisfied.

- the child's parents are dead and there is no guardian or custodian to look after the child

- the child has been abandoned by his or her parents

- the child's parent suffers from some permanent disability which makes the parent incapable of looking after the child

- the parent is of such habits or mode of life as to be unfit to have the care of the child

- the parent has consistently failed without reasonable cause to discharge the obligations of a parent

- there is already a Parental Rights Resolution in force in relation to one parent who is, or is likely to become, a member of the household comprising the child and his other parent

- the child has been in voluntary care for three years

If the local authority's social workers wish to pass a Parental Rights Resolution they will make a report to the social services committee. The local authority must then arrange either for the parents to attend the meeting so that they can put their views to the councillors, or arrange for the parents to put their views in writing to the committee. There is no formal procedure for taking the child's wishes into account.

The local authority must notify the parents in writing once it has passed a Parental Rights Resolution and tell them of their right to object to it. Parents have 28 days to object. If they do, the local authority can either let the resolution lapse, or notify the juvenile court and start court proceedings. If court proceedings are started the resolution will remain in force until the court has heard the case. The authority must start court proceedings within 14 days of receiving the parents' objection or the resolution will lapse.

If the case comes before the juvenile court the court must decide whether the resolution should continue. It can only do this if it is satisfied on *all* the following counts:

- that grounds for the resolution existed at the time that it was passed

- that grounds still exist at the time of the juvenile court hearing

- that it is in the child's interests that the resolution should continue to exist

In proceedings in the juvenile court the parents are parties to the proceedings and are entitled to apply for legal aid.

The representation of the child

Children have no automatic right to be represented in parental rights proceedings. If their interests are thought to be different from those of their parents the court can make the child a party as well and appoint a *Guardian ad litem* to represent the child in the same way as in care proceedings.

Ending a Parental Rights Resolution

A parent or child can ask the local authority to revoke a Parental Rights Resolution and the local authority will do so if it thinks that it will be for the benefit of the child. The local authority can revoke the resolution without going back to court. A parent, but not the child, can apply to the juvenile court to revoke a Parental Rights Resolution.

The court should revoke the resolution if it is satisfied that there were no grounds for passing the resolution or that the resolution should be rescinded in the interests of the child. The first of these two grounds is only available within the first six months after the resolution was passed. After that time a parent wishing to apply to the court to have the resolution rescinded must show the court that it is in the interests of the child to do so.

Appeals

Appeals can be made by the parent or the local authority from the juvenile court to the family division of the High Court. The child or the *Guardian ad litem* can appeal, too, but only if the child has been made a party to the proceedings.

Effect of a care order

A care order places a child in the care of the local authority and the law gives the local authority very wide powers to decide how the child should be brought up and where the child should live. It also imposes powers and duties on local authorities.

Parents have few rights when their children are in care under an order. They must notify the local authority of any change in their address but the local authority does not have to tell them the child's address. In addition, anyone who removes or helps to remove a child from care without the consent of the local authority commits an offence.

The duties of local authorities towards children in care

When making any decision about a child in care the local authority must put the child's welfare first. It should also give consideration to the child's wishes and feelings. It can ignore these considerations if it thinks it is necessary to do so to protect members of the public or to comply with a direction given by a Secretary of State in relation to any particular child. The local authority's view of what is best for the child will not necessarily be the child's view or the parents' views. This often causes problems for all concerned.

The child has the right to have his or her case reviewed every six months if a care order has been made. During the course of the review the local authority should consider whether or not to make an application for the care order to be discharged. There is no standard procedure laid down for carrying out reviews and practice varies enormously. In some local authorities the parents and/or child will be asked to come to the review. Some authorities' reviews simply consist of meetings of the social workers concerned.

It can be difficult for children in care to make their views felt. If they are dissatisfied with the way they are being treated they can complain to the authority or try to get their parents to take action on their behalf. A child in care could also seek the assistance of the Children's Legal Centre or the National Association of Young People in Care (see page 195). Alternatively a child could consult a solicitor. Local authorities should not stop children and young people getting legal advice.

Accommodation

The local authority is responsible for providing accommodation for the child. This varies, but generally the local authority has complete discretion as to where the child should be placed. There are, however, exceptions to this (see page 185 for example).

The usual types of accommodation provided by the local authority are children's homes, foster homes or specialist units. Children in care are often placed at home with their parents although the court has the power to restrict this if a child is in care because of committing an offence (see page 184).

As far as possible the accommodation should be near to the child's own home. There are three main types of children's homes all of which are subject to different regulations.

COMMUNITY HOMES

Most community homes are owned and run by local authorities. Although some are owned by other organizations, the local authority will have a say in how the home is run.

Children who live in community homes usually go from the home to local schools. However, some have education provided on the premises. Such homes are called Community Homes with Education (CHE).

VOLUNTARY HOMES

Most voluntary homes are owned by voluntary bodies such as the National Children's Homes or particular trusts. Many are especially designed to cater for children with particular needs, for example, children who are blind or handicapped, or are suffering from forms of mental illness or disturbance.

All voluntary homes must be registered with the Secretary of State who lays down how many children can live in the home, the standard of accommodation and equipment, and the way the home is managed. A home which fails to register or to comply with the regulations can be closed by the local authority. Local authorities have the duty to visit all voluntary homes within their area. A child in the care of a local authority outside the area where the home is can be visited by his or her own social worker.

Registration and inspection are not sufficient to ensure that homes are properly run. Although many are excellent some fall below acceptable standards.

PRIVATE HOMES

There are approximately 170 private homes in England and Wales. These are run by individuals, not by local authorities or voluntary organizations. At present they are not subject to any regulations although there are proposals for them to be registered. As with voluntary homes some homes have been shown to provide poor standards of accommodation and care. Controls are long overdue.

FOSTER PARENTS

Children in care can be placed with foster parents approved by the local authority. Foster parents are under the overall control of the local authority although in practice there is more give and take. The local authority must visit the child in the foster home.

Foster parents do not have to live in the same area as the child's own parents and often do not, with the result that the child may end up living some distance away from his or her natural family.

The major decisions about the child, such as whether or not he or she should return home or have access to the parents, should be taken by the local authority. Day-to-day decisions about how the child should dress and what he or she should eat will be taken by the foster parents.

Foster parents should not, however, cause the child to be brought up in a different religion, although in practice many foster parents do take their foster children to their own church regardless of the parents' wishes.

Foster parents are paid an allowance by the local authority. This varies from authority to authority, increasing as the child gets older. In some circumstances foster parents can apply for custodianship orders (see page 77), which will give them rights over the child and reduce those of the authority. Foster parents sometimes apply to adopt foster children in their care.

Maintenance for children in care

The local authority has a duty to maintain a child in its care. It does, however, have the right to demand a contribution from the child's parents, if the child is under 16, or from the child if the child is over 16.

The local authority cannot usually demand a contribution from the father of an illegitimate child. Sometimes, though, the local authority can apply for an affiliation order or, if one is in force, arrange for the maintenance to be paid to the authority (see page 37). The authority cannot ask for a contribution from parents or a child who are in receipt of supplementary benefit or family income supplement. The maximum contribution payable is the amount that the authority pays to foster parents in its area.

If the local authority wishes to ask for a contribution it must serve the parents with a notice stating the amount of the contribution asked for. If agreement cannot be reached between the parent and the local authority within a month, or if agreement is reached but the parent does not make the agreed payments, the local authority can apply to the magistrates' court for a contribution order. The court can make what order it thinks is reasonable subject to the upper limit. These rules also apply to children where contributions are sought from them. A contribution order remains in force as long as the child is in the care of the local authority. If the child is in care but living with parents the local authority cannot request a contribution.

Contribution orders can be enforced by the court if they are not paid. Usually this would be by an attachment of earnings order requiring the parent's employer to deduct a specified amount from that person's wages before they are paid. They can also be enforced by taking away property to the value of the amount. This is known as 'distress'. In the last resort they can be enforced by imprisonment if no other way seems appropriate.

Education

If a local authority has the care of the child it has the same duty as a parent to ensure that the child receives efficient full-time education suitable to the child's age, ability and aptitude and special educational needs. This duty extends to foster parents who are looking after the child or those in charge of the children's home where the child is living.

Medical treatment

A local authority has a duty to ensure that the child receives medical attention and treatment if necessary. Children's homes, other than private homes, must arrange medical and dental care for children living there and must make sure that the home has a reasonable standard of hygiene.

A child should be medically examined before or shortly after going to live in a foster home and once there, at least every six months if the child is under two years old and once a year if older. All foster parents are required to give an undertaking to the local authority to consult a doctor whenever a child is ill and allow the child to be medically examined whenever the local authority requires it.

If a child is in care under a care order the local authority has the power to consent on the child's behalf to any medical treatment where parental consent would be required, for example, surgery or a blood transfusion. If the child is seriously ill or has suffered a serious injury then the parent is entitled to be informed.

Religion

The local authority cannot change a child's religion or allow the child to be brought up in any religious belief other than the child's own. Foster parents are required to undertake to allow the child to practise his or her religion.

It can be difficult to decide what religious belief the child has. Normally this will be the same as the parents. If the parents have different religions it could be either religion. The local authority should give the child's wishes consideration, although there is no law which says at what age a child acquires the right to choose his or her own religious belief.

Discipline

The person looking after the child, that is the local authority, foster parent, or children's home, has the right to exercise reasonable discipline over the child. Such reasonable discipline can include corporal punishment. Where a child is placed in a residential home, the power of those in charge of the home to impose physical punishment is very strictly controlled.

The law forbids corporal punishment in voluntary homes for any girl over the age of 10 or any boy over the age of 16. If a child is under 10 he or she may be smacked on the hand; if the child is a boy over 10 years old he may be given six strokes of the cane on the buttocks over his ordinary clothing. No other form of physical punishment may be administered.

There are no specific regulations regarding corporal punishment in community homes. However, the local authority authorizes the range of punishments to be applied in its homes and practice varies widely. If punishment is administered in a community home a record of this must be kept.

Local authorities may limit the powers that foster parents have in relation to discipline. If there are no such instructions, foster parents will have the same powers as parents.

Restricting the child's liberty

In general, local authorities are not allowed to restrict a child's liberty. This means that a child cannot be locked in a single room or confined to a certain section of a home. A continuous fence or wall around a community home which is more than 6 ft (180 cm) in height cannot be built without the approval of the Secretary of State. This does not prevent the home locking windows and outside gates and doors to prevent intruders getting in, but it must do so in such a way that children are not prevented from going out during the daytime.

There are exceptions to this. The first is that a child may be kept in secure accommodation for up to 72 hours consecutively, or for up to 72 hours in any period of 28 days. If the 72-hour period ends on a Saturday, Sunday or public holiday it is automatically extended to midday on the first working day afterwards. The local authority must give consideration to the child's needs and welfare, and then can only deprive children of their liberty if the following conditions are met:

● the child has a history of absconding and is likely to abscond from any other sort of accommodation; and

● if the child absconds, it is likely that his or her physical, mental or moral welfare will be at risk; or

● that if he or she is kept in any other form of accommodation he or she is likely to injure himself or herself or other people.

SECURE ACCOMMODATION ORDERS

If the local authority wishes to detain a child for longer than 72 hours in secure accommodation it must apply to the juvenile court for an order allowing it to do so. The court has to find the same conditions proved as set out previously.

The child has the right to go to court and be represented by a solicitor, as do the child's parents. The court cannot usually make a secure accommodation order unless the child is legally represented. If the court finds that the grounds exist for restricting the child's liberty, it can make an order enabling the local authority to keep the child in secure accommodation for up to three months. If the local authority wish to extend that time it has to apply to the juvenile court who may extend their authority for further periods of up to six months.

The fact that the juvenile court has made an order does not mean that the local authority has to place the child in secure accommodation. The local authority should not keep the child in secure accommodation after the grounds cease to apply even if the order is still in force. The child and the local authority can appeal to the crown court against the decision of the juvenile court.

If a child is detained in secure accommodation the local authority has to appoint at least two people to review the child's case at least every three months. The review has to consider whether the grounds for keeping the child in secure accommodation continue to exist and whether the placement is appropriate. At the review the views of the child and the child's parents must be taken into account, as well as the views of anybody who has had the care of the child and the local authority.

Many children who are detained in secure accommodation are said to be disturbed and as a result may be administered tranquillizing medicines. The administration of these is governed by guidelines which state that such drugs can only be administered on clinical and therapeutic grounds in cases where there is no other method of dealing with the child or the child is at imminent risk of harming himself or others.

Access

Usually the local authority has the right to control access by the child to his or her parents or anybody else. There are certain exceptions. Where the child is in voluntary care the local authority should not stop parents seeing their child. If the child is in care as a result of custody proceedings in the High Court or county court or wardship proceedings, the court can make orders saying when and to whom the child should have access. Parents have the right to apply to the court for access if it is refused. The court doesn't have to make an access order and can leave access to the discretion of the local authority.

The Department of Health and Social Security has published a code of practice called *Access to Children in Care*. This lays down certain basic principles for local authorities. The local authority should normally arrange access for parents and this should be on a regular basis in a setting which is as informal as possible.

Parents and children have no right to apply to the court because they are dissatisfied with the arrangements made by the local authority for access, unless the care order was made in divorce or wardship proceedings, or in custody proceedings in the High Court.

IF THE LOCAL AUTHORITY STOPS ACCESS

If the local authority decides to stop access then the parents, but
not the child, can apply to the juvenile court for an access order.
This applies where the child is in care as a result of care
proceedings, or custody proceedings in the magistrates' court or
the county court, or under a Parental Rights Resolution.

If the local authority decides to stop access it must tell the parents
and inform them of their right to apply for an access order. A
parent must apply to the juvenile court within six months of
receiving the notice.

At the hearing the child can be made a party to the proceedings
and a *Guardian ad litem* can be appointed to represent the child's
interests (see page 60). The *Guardian ad litem* can then appoint a
solicitor to act for the child. Legal aid is available for both the
parent and the child.

The court must decide about access on the basis of what is best
for the child. It will hear the evidence and views of the local
authority, the parent, the child and the *Guardian ad litem* and can
make an order requiring the local authority to give the parents
access to the child. The order can specify where access is to take
place, how often it is to take place and how long it is to last. Once
an order has been made the local authority is not allowed to vary
the arrangements, except in emergencies, without the agreement
of the juvenile court. The court can refuse to make an access order.
Both the local authority and the child's parents can apply to
change the order.

Where an access order has been made the local authority can apply
for the order to be suspended for up to seven days in an
emergency. If the authority then applies to change the order the
order will be suspended until the application has been heard.
Before suspending access the magistrates must be satisfied that if
access continued the child would be seriously at risk.

The child's parents, the local authority and the child, if the child
has been made a party to the application, can appeal to the family
division of the High Court, against a decision of the juvenile court
about access.

Adoption

Under English law an adoption order cannot be made unless either the child's parents consent or the court dispenses with their consent (see page 49). A local authority does not have the right to consent to the adoption of a child or to an order freeing the child for adoption.

Parental contact

Parents of a child in care have a duty to keep the local authority informed about where they are living. Not to do so is a criminal offence, punishable by a fine.

Emigration

The local authority cannot arrange for a child's emigration without the consent of the Secretary of State. The Secretary of State will only consent if satisfied that:

- emigration would be of benefit to the child

- suitable arrangements have been made or will be made for the child in the new country

- the child's parents or guardians have been consulted, or that it is not practicable to do so

- the child consents. In the case of a child who is too young to give an opinion the Secretary of State can consent on the child's behalf if the parents, guardian, relative or friend are also emigrating to join the child.

Before giving consent the Secretary of State will require a great deal of information. In particular he will want to know about the conditions in the place where the child is going to live, some background history of the child and his family, the parents' views, and information about the type of social work help available in the new country.

Passport

If a child needs a passport to go abroad then normally the consent of the child's parents would be required. If a child is in compulsory care the consent of the local authority would be sufficient.

Consent to marriage

Where a child is the subject of a Parental Rights Resolution, the local authority can consent to the child's marriage if the child is between 16 and 18 years old. If the child is subject to a care order then normally the local authority and the parents will have to consent, although the law is not very clear on this.

Supervision orders

Supervision orders can be made in care, wardship, custody or divorce proceedings. They can also be made in criminal proceedings but this section does not apply to these.

A supervision order can only last for up to three years if made in care proceedings and must end on the child's eighteenth birthday. Under a supervision order the child will usually remain at home although conditions can be put in requiring the child to live elsewhere (see page 183).

Supervision orders place the child under the supervision of a social worker. A probation officer can supervise if the child is over 13, or if the child is under 13 can do so if a probation officer is already involved with the family. A supervision order does not entitle the supervisor to enter the child's home or remove the child.

Either the supervisor or the child can apply to have the order discharged. The court can either discharge it or make a care order.

Wardship

Wardship is a very old procedure in which the High Court acquires legal custody of the child. This does not mean that the High Court actually looks after the child but that it has very great powers to decide how the child should be brought up.

Wardship proceedings are often used by people other than parents. Grandparents or relatives, for example, if they feel the child is not being properly looked after by its parents, may take this action. Sometimes, although not as much as used to be the case, such proceedings may be brought by parents of older children, particularly if they disapprove of their daughter's association with a boyfriend. They are often used by one parent to prevent the child being snatched out of the country by the other parent.

These proceedings are not only brought in cases where there are disputes between parents. They are often a means whereby local authorities can obtain a care order when, for technical reasons, they could not obtain such an order from a juvenile court.

Conditions

Any unmarried child who is under 18 and has some connection with England and Wales can be made a ward of court. This means that a child who lives in England and Wales can be made a ward of court even though he or she is not a British subject. The court cannot, however, act where the child's parents claim diplomatic immunity, or when the Home Office is considering deportation of the child's parents, and will not usually do so where a child has been refused admission to the country by the immigration authorities.

Procedure

Wardship proceedings are heard in High Court, Family Division—either in London or in one of the district registries situated up and down the country.

Anyone who has a connection with a child or is concerned about the child can make a child a ward of court. The procedure is very simple. It involves completing a form obtainable from the High Court or one of the High Court district registries. This should be sent to the court with the fee, currently £60.

Once wardship proceedings have been started anyone who has an interest in or is concerned about the child can be joined as a party to the proceedings. This includes the child. If the child does take part representation will usually be by the Official Solicitor (see page 12).

Sometimes children themselves have started wardship proceedings. If they do, they will need an adult to act as their *Guardian ad litem*. An example of such a case occurred when a teenage girl's father and step-mother separated. The step-mother started divorce proceedings and obtained a custody order. The girl did not want to live with her step-mother but with her father. The judge who decided the custody case would not even see the girl. The girl obtained legal help and made herself a ward of court. The wardship court ordered that the girl should live with her father and this superseded the earlier custody order.

Apart from the form, it is not necessary to lodge any other documents when starting the proceedings, although the court will want to have a copy of the child's birth certificate if that is available. The court will also wish to know the whereabouts of the child if possible.

After the child has been made a ward of court it is necessary to take out an 'application for directions' to be given by the court. This application must be taken out within 21 days of making the child a ward of court. The child will then remain a ward of court until the application for directions is heard, even if this is later than 21 days. Alternatively an application can be made to a judge. This is normally the case if an emergency order is sought, for example, to stop the child leaving the country. On such an application the judge would normally confirm that the child is a ward of court. If neither of these steps is taken the child ceases to be a ward of court after 21 days.

In an emergency an application can be made to the court immediately.

Orders that the court can make

The court can make almost any order that is necessary to protect the child. It can grant care and control of the child to a parent, grandparent, uncle, aunt or other relative, or family friend. It can also make an order committing the child to the care of the local authority. It will do this if it thinks there are circumstances which make it impracticable or undesirable for the child to live at home. Today, wardship proceedings are often used by local authorities who want to take a child into care but who feel that the rules in the juvenile court make it unlikely they would get a care order there.

The court can make an order permitting someone to start adoption proceedings (see page 45). It can also make wide-ranging orders about access to the child, even if the child has been made the subject of a care order.

Consequences of wardship

While the child is a ward of court, no major steps can be taken in the child's life without the consent of the court. In particular the court's permission is needed before:

- the child moves home

- the child goes to live with someone else

- the child leaves England or Wales or travels abroad even for a holiday or day trip

- the child has any medical treatment or sees a psychiatrist. This does not include routine visits to the doctor or dentist.

- the child gets married

- anybody applies to adopt the child

- the child can be known by a different name

- there is any publicity about the child

Sometimes emergencies arise which mean that it is not possible to get the High Court's permission before the change takes place, for example, if the parent who is looking after the child abandons the child or dies. In cases such as this the High Court should be notified as soon as possible.

Custodianship

Custodianship is a new procedure which enables people other than a child's parents to apply to the court for legal custody of the child, secure the child's legal position in their home, and their own legal status in relation to the child. It gives the legal custody of a child to the person who has the order. This means that the custodian has the same rights and duties as a parent (see page 18). A custodian can consent to the marriage of a child between 16 and 18 and consent to medical treatment on the child's behalf.

However, a custodian cannot consent to a child's adoption or emigration, or change the child's name.

A custodianship order can be made in respect of any child under 18. It ceases to have effect when the child reaches 18. The order can subsequently be revoked by the courts.

A great criticism of the custodianship provisions is that the child has no real rights to take part in the application or to apply to the court for an order or for the revocation of an order. The child's rights to have his or her view put to the court are limited also and not enforceable. As this procedure has only recently come into force it is difficult to predict how much it will be used.

Conditions

The child must have been living in the person's home for a certain period of time before the application can be made. This varies according to the circumstances:

- three months if the person making the application is a relative, that is grandparent, brother, sister, uncle or aunt or step-parent of the child and the person who has custody already agrees to the application

- 12 months where the person making the application is not a relative or step-parent and the person with legal custody agrees

- three years in any case where the person with legal custody does not agree

Who may apply

The application can be made by anyone who meets the conditions but not by:

- a biological parent. They can apply for a custody order in other proceedings (see Chapter 2).

- a step-parent where there is a divorce court order giving custody to the biological parent

The procedure can be used by foster parents and relatives who have been looking after a child but who have no legal rights if the parent suddenly wants to take the child.

Procedure

The application can be made to the High Court, county court or magistrates' court. It is up to the person making the application to decide which. Where the case is very difficult, the magistrates' court is not really suitable, and the application should be made in the High Court or county court.

Before the court can decide whether or not to make a custody order it must obtain a report from the local authority for the area where the child lives. The social services department will then investigate all the circumstances and will want to see the person making the application, the person with custody of the child and the child itself.

When coming to a decision the court must place the child's interests first. However, the court does not have to hear from the child at all.

Orders the court can make

If the court makes the custody order it can also order that the mother, father, grandparent or a person that the child has lived with should have access to the child. It can also order that the mother and father contribute towards the child's maintenance. A custodian can apply for an affiliation order to establish who the child's father is. The court can also order that the child is not taken out of England and Wales without the court's permission. A custody order can be made even though the child is in the care of the local authority, if say, he or she is living with foster parents. In this case the foster parents may lose their fostering allowance paid by the local authority.

If the child is not in care, the court can make an order committing the child to the care of the local authority, or can make a supervision order if it thinks that the circumstances justify it. It would only do this if it felt that the child should not continue to live with the person making the application.

The court can make a custodianship order in adoption proceedings if it feels that although the legal requirements for an adoption order are met, custodianship is a better alternative. It will then grant custody to the people who made the adoption application. It seems that the courts may do this where a parent has continued to see the child even after it has gone to live with the people applying to adopt it.

Revoking a custodianship order

A custodian, parent or local authority, but not the child, can apply to revoke a custodianship order. Usually the court will have to have a written report from the local authority or probation officer as to the desirability of the new arrangements proposed for the child.

When application is made to revoke a custodianship order the court does not have to be told of the child's wishes or feelings as is the case when an order is made. This is an unfortunate omission as the consequences for a child of the revocation of the order may well be more serious than the effects of it being made.

At the hearing the court must make a care order if, after the custodianship order was revoked, no one would have legal custody of the child, or if the court does not think that the child should be in the custody of the person who would be entitled to it if the order is revoked.

Guardianship

A guardian is someone who is in most respects placed in the position of a parent. A guardian is entitled to look after the child, make decisions about the child's life and administer the child's property. A guardian can also give consent to the child's marriage or adoption.

Guardians are not the same as *Guardians ad litem* (see page 60). Although many guardians are appointed, few are ever called upon to act as such, probably because most parents live until their children become 18.

Children normally only have guardians if one or both of their parents have died. If the child is legitimate and one parent dies, the surviving parent will become the child's guardian.

Both the child's parents have equal rights to appoint a guardian to look after the child after they die. This can be done either by will or by deed. If the parent who has died has appointed a guardian in his or her will, the surviving parent will become the guardian of the child jointly with the named guardian. If the surviving parent objects to the guardian appointed in the will, the guardian ceases to act. Adoptive parents can appoint guardians in the same way as natural parents.

The position of an illegitimate child is different. Only the mother has the power to appoint a guardian. If the father has obtained a custody order in respect of the child he can appoint a guardian.

Alternatively the court can appoint a guardian to look after a child. It can also resolve disputes between guardians. This is most likely to happen where the child has no parent or guardian and the person who wants to look after the child or is looking after the child applies to the court for the appointment.

The court always has the power to remove or replace guardians.

6 Education

Most children go to state schools. The state system is free to the extent that schools cannot charge for extra lessons—such as special music lessons, which are usually 'extras' in the private system (see page 95). Uniforms and some equipment may not be free, although grants and financial assistance may be available (see page 127). This section describes the major components of the state system of education.

The Secretary of State

The Secretary of State for Education has overall responsibility for the organization of education, with control over many of the arrangements made by local education authorities (LEAs). The minister can intervene to change arrangements made by them if these seem unreasonable.

Perhaps the most important part of the Secretary of State's job is to set the overall framework for education. For example, it was a Secretary of State who ordered all LEAs to formulate plans for a secondary comprehensive education service and it was another Secretary of State from a government of different political persuasion who ordered that to cease.

It is the Secretary of State who has introduced the new GCSE exams. Central government through the Secretary of State can exert control of LEAs' budgets.

The Secretary of State's responsibilities include promoting educational services throughout the country but do not extend to laying down detailed guidelines as to what should be taught in schools; this is the task of the LEAs and the schools themselves.

The Secretary of State can arbitrate in certain disputes between parents and the LEA, such as disagreements over which school a child is to attend, and whether a child should undergo a medical examination. He can also intervene in disputes which may arise between a LEA and school governors. Whenever the Secretary of State intervenes his decision is final and could only be altered by the courts if they were satisfied that he had not acted fairly or properly.

Local education authorities (LEAs)

The country is divided into local education authorities which cover the same areas as county councils or district councils, except for the inner London boroughs which have a separate education authority, the Inner London Education Authority (ILEA). LEAs are managed by education committees, the majority of whose members must be elected councillors, although there is a power to appoint other members as well. Their meetings must be held in public. The authority itself is run by officers headed by a Chief Education Officer. The exact powers of LEAs are redefined from time to time by central government.

The law imposes duties on LEAs to provide sufficient schools for all primary and secondary pupils in their area as well as to make provision for further education for pupils up to the age of 19 who want it. Primary education ends at between $10\frac{1}{2}$ years and 12 years, and secondary education continues from $10\frac{1}{2}$ or 12 years until children reach 16.

The way in which schools are organized varies from authority to authority, and from school to school. Some LEAs divide schools into three groups—primary, middle and higher schools—and some have just primary and secondary schools. Some authorities maintain a system of grammar schools and secondary schools for secondary education, with admittance to grammar school depending on the results of an examination. Others have a comprehensive system which provides for the admittance of all pupils to secondary schools without having an examination to decide which school they should go to. Until recently there was an obligation on all education authorities to make arrangements for the provision of comprehensive education. This is no longer so.

LEAs can also provide boarding school accommodation where it is necessary in order to provide adequate educational facilities. Some authorities may need to provide board and lodging accommodation for children who have to travel too far to school. A parental contribution or even a contribution from the pupil may sometimes be required for this. LEAs also have a duty to provide proper facilities for children with special educational needs (see page 94).

LEAs are not obliged to provide nursery education for children under five years old but have the power to do so. Many provide separate nursery schools or educational facilities in day nurseries. These will usually only be available to children or families with special needs or difficulties—it is always worth checking, though.

The LEA also has a responsibility to provide facilities for recreation, social and physical training.

Schools

There are two main types of school providing education in the state sector.

COUNTY SCHOOLS

These are the state schools which have been set up by the LEAs and are run by them.

VOLUNTARY SCHOOLS

These can be either primary or secondary schools. They are maintained by the local education authority but were not established by them. They include, for example, church schools.

School governors

Schools are under the day-to-day control of a headteacher, but all must have governing bodies. The governors act in accordance with an 'Instrument of Government', which every school must have, and which, among other things, allocates responsibility to the governing body for certain tasks. The exact responsibilities delegated to the governors vary from school to school and area to area.

Governing bodies of schools must include governors appointed by the LEA, the headteacher, unless the headteacher does not wish to be a governor, at least two parents and one or two teachers, depending on the size of the school. Governors often have responsibilities for the appointment of the headteacher and for various matters to do with discipline. A few schools also have pupil governors but the right to have pupil governors may soon be abolished. The frequency with which the governors meet varies from school to school.

Parents' duties

The law says that parents must ensure that their children of compulsory school age receive efficient, full-time education suitable to their age, ability and aptitude or to meet any special needs that they may have. The law does not say that children have to be educated at school but if their child is registered at school parents have a duty to ensure that the child attends regularly. 'Parent' includes for these purposes anybody who has actual custody of the child.

Compulsory school age

A child becomes of compulsory school age at the age of five. Parents cannot insist on their child being admitted before his or her fifth birthday although many LEAs and schools admit children at the beginning of the term before their fifth birthday. A child remains of compulsory school age until the age of 16. This does not mean that a child can lawfully leave school on his or her sixteenth birthday.

A child can leave school at the end of the spring term if the child's sixteenth birthday is between 1 September and 31 January. If the child's birthday is between 31 January and 1 September he or she can leave on the May school-leaving date (the Friday before the last Monday in May).

Efficient full-time education

6The law does not define this condition. Disputes sometimes arise between parents and LEAs, particularly where parents wish to educate their children at home. If the LEA is not satisfied that a child is receiving efficient full-time education it can serve a notice on the parents followed by a school attendance order, and may even bring care proceedings.

LEAs have wide powers to ensure that a child does receive efficient full time education. There are three main procedures: making a school attendance order, prosecuting the parents and bringing care proceedings.

SCHOOL ATTENDANCE ORDERS

If the education authority feels that a child is not receiving efficient full-time education it must serve the child's parents with a notice. This requires the parent to show that the child is receiving a proper education, whether by regular attendance at school or otherwise. If the parent does not do this to the LEA's satisfaction, it can make a school attendance order which requires the parent to register the child at a named school. A parent has an opportunity after the notice is served to choose the school. The local authority has to accept that choice unless it considers the school is unsuitable for the child, or that the child's attendance would prejudice the provision of efficient education or the efficient use of resources.

Failure to comply with a school attendance order is an offence for which parents can be prosecuted and fined. On a third or subsequent conviction the court has the power to send a parent to prison.

PROSECUTING PARENTS

Parents can also be prosecuted when a child is a registered pupil at the school but fails to attend. This should not be done if the school has given the child permission to be absent or the child is prevented from attending because of illness or any unavoidable cause. An unavoidable cause can be that the school is not within walking distance and that the local education authority has not made suitable arrangements for transport or for boarding accommodation.

If the parents are convicted the court can fine them and on a third or subsequent conviction can impose a sentence of imprisonment.

CARE PROCEEDINGS

If a child is not receiving a proper education the LEA can bring care proceedings. The procedure is the same as that described on page 57. If the court is satisfied that the child is not being properly educated it can make a care order. Before making such an order the court must be satisfied not only that the child is not receiving full-time education but is also in need of care and control, which he or she would not receive unless an order was made. The courts have held that the second condition is satisfied by proving that the child is not receiving education.

If a care order is made the child is committed to the care of the local authority and not the local education authority (see Chapter 5).

Choice of school

Parents, but not children, have a considerable say in what school their child should go to. The law says that as far as possible the LEA must make arrangements so that parents can make an informed choice about their children's school. To help parents do this, LEAs must publish particulars of each school, giving details of the arrangements for the admission of pupils. These details must include:

- the numbers of pupils that the authority or the school governors intend to admit in each school year

- the different tasks of the authority and the governors in relation to the school

- the school's admissions policy

- the arrangements for pupils who do not live in the area

- the criteria for offering places at schools which are not maintained by the authority

- the school's links with any particular religious domination

- transfer arrangements

- policies in respect of transport, school uniforms, meals and other refreshments and public examinations

- special educational provisions for pupils with special educational needs

- in Wales, arrangements and policies as regards the use of the Welsh language.

When the child's parents have chosen a school the LEA and the school must accept this *unless*:

● compliance would prejudice the provision of efficient education or the efficient use of resources

● the school chosen is not one maintained by the local authority, and compliance would interfere with admission arrangements made between the authority and the governors

● selection at the school chosen is made by reference to ability or aptitude and compliance would be incompatible with those arrangements. This would apply, for example, where the school only admitted pupils who had passed an eleven-plus exam.

A parent whose preference is not accepted has a right of appeal. The LEA or school governors have to arrange for an appeal committee to be set up. The appeal committee's decision is binding on the LEA, the governors of the school and the parents.

How schools are organized

Schools vary as to how they are organized and the law gives them considerable discretion. However, there are certain rules with which all LEAs and state schools have to comply.

Starting times and holidays

The LEA, or sometimes the school governors, have power, subject to certain limits, to decide when the school day starts and ends and when terms begin and end. The minimum length of the school day must normally be three hours of teaching, not including religious instruction, for pupils under eight and at least four hours of teaching, not including religious instruction, for children aged eight or over.

The school day has to consist of two sessions separated by a break. Some schools have classes on Saturday mornings, in which case they can have two days when there is only one session. A school must meet for at least 400 sessions per year—a session is half a day—although up to 20 sessions can be deducted for occasional school holidays.

What is taught

Unlike some other countries, the British education system does not lay down a detailed syllabus for all subjects and leaves this largely up to the discretion of the LEA and the school. What is taught is, however, subject to conditions imposed by Inspectors of Education where they feel it necessary.

The exception is religious education and worship. The law provides that the school day in every state school and voluntary school must begin with an act of collective worship which must normally take place on the school premises. The form of religious worship varies and can be non-denominational. In some voluntary schools it follows the religious forms dictated by the school's founders.

A child cannot be excused from attendance at religious worship unless his or her parents request it. If they do, that request must be honoured. The child has no right to request to be excused from attending.

The law also provides that religious instruction must be given in every county and voluntary school. Again, a parent can request that his or her child does not receive religious instruction. If the LEA is satisfied that arrangements have been made for the child to receive religious instruction during school hours elsewhere, the child may be withdrawn from the school for that to take place, as long as this is reasonable and the school does not provide that type of religious instruction.

Discipline and punishment

The subject of discipline and punishment at school, particularly corporal punishment, has long been a controversial one. In 1982 the British government was held to be in breach of the European Convention on Human Rights by not respecting parents' objections to corporal punishment in state schools. Recently, the government attempted to change the law to comply with the European Court decision and give parents the right to stop schools inflicting corporal punishment. However, this measure was defeated and has not been reintroduced.

While at school or under the responsibility of the school, for example, on a school trip, legal responsibility for the child rests with the headteacher who is, in law, acting as the parent. This means that the headteacher has the power to punish the child if that is in the child's interests or is necessary to maintain discipline in the interests of the school as a whole. This right can be extended to an assistant teacher. This right can also mean that a child who is not properly dressed can be expelled.

Just as a parent has the right to inflict moderate and reasonable corporal punishment, so does a headteacher. What is moderate and reasonable has not been defined, but if punishment is excessive or unreasonably administered it would constitute assault, for which an action for damages would be possible. Following the European court's decision it is doubtful whether a school could inflict corporal punishment against a parent's wishes or expel a child because his or her parents objected to corporal punishment for the child.

Detention—that is keeping the child at school when others have left—is a common form of punishment. Again the teacher has the power to do this so long as the detention is reasonable. Whether or not it is reasonable will be affected by the attitude of the child's parents, the age of the child concerned and the risks attached to the child travelling home at an unusual hour. Schools should notify parents in advance if they are going to detain their children. Excessive or unreasonable detention could lead the parents taking out an injunction to stop it happening again and possibly suing for damages.

Expulsion and suspension

A pupil in a state school may be expelled by the authority or by the school governors. The pupil's name is then removed from the school register. Expulsion is relatively rare. The law is not very clear but it seems that expulsion must be used sparingly and only in exceptional circumstances. The parents of a pupil who is expelled can appeal to the Secretary of State for Education or, in Wales, to the Secretary of State for Wales. If the Secretary of State decides that the child was expelled unreasonably then the child must be re-admitted to the school. If that does not happen then the LEA must arrange for efficient full-time education for the pupil and make alternative arrangements.

Suspension presents more difficult problems since, if a child is suspended, he or she will remain on the register of the school and will probably not be able to go to another school. If the suspension is for an indefinite period of time, the authority should take some action. If the suspension occurs because, for example, the child is not properly dressed then the education authority may wish to take steps to ensure that the parent complies with the relevant rules. If the suspension is for behaviour during school hours then, unless it is for a short period of time only, the authority must make arrangements for the child to receive education.

Medical and dental inspections

By law there must be regular medical and dental inspections of pupils at schools. LEAs have to make arrangements for these. A parent can, however, object to his or her child being examined and the education authority must abide by this objection.

The Secretary of State can also, in certain circumstances, require that a pupil be medically examined, in which case the parent has to be served with a notice. If the notice is not complied with, the parent can be prosecuted and fined if convicted. This provision also applies to pupils in colleges of further education, in which case the notice can be served on the pupil.

Milk and meals

The school meals service was, until recently, a highly organized affair. All schools had to provide cooked midday meals for pupils. The dietary requirements of such meals were the subject of detailed instructions and were meant to provide a balanced diet and a suitable main meal. Now it is up to the LEA whether it provides a school meals service. The authority may charge for this. All schools, however, have to provide appropriate facilities for pupils to consume food on the premises, and appropriate meals for children whose parents are on supplementary benefit or low incomes. School milk does not have to be provided but some local education authorities do.

In special schools the governors have to provide, free of charge, milk and a meal or some other refreshment for pupils whose parents receive supplementary benefit or family income supplement. In schools where milk, meals or other refreshments are provided the governing body of the school can make arrangements not to charge parents.

Uniform

LEAs are able to provide clothing for pupils and also clothing for physical training. They can charge for this but may not if the parent would suffer hardship as a result (see page 127).

Care of pupils

Schools must exercise proper care of pupils in their charge. If children are injured as a result of the negligence of teachers and staff, the LEA can be liable for the damage that is caused. The same applies to injuries caused to third people as a result of negligent supervision. If, for example, while on a school outing a teacher neglects to supervise a child so that an accident is caused and a road user is injured then the education authority can be liable.

The duty to take care of pupils extends to injuries caused to the child by itself. For example, in a case where a child who was sent by a teacher to deal with a fire in a school and was injured, the education authority was held to be liable.

Discrimination in education

It is unlawful to discriminate on the grounds of sex, race or ethnic origin in the provision of educational facilities. This applies to schools, the facilities offered in them and to vocational training bodies. LEAs have the general duty to ensure that educational facilities are provided without sex or racial discrimination.

As far as racial discrimination is concerned, it is also the duty of every local education authority to make sure that it encourages the elimination of unlawful racial discrimination and promotes equality of opportunity and good relations between people of different racial groups.

Discrimination can be either direct or indirect. Direct discrimination occurs where a person is treated less favourably because of their colour or sex. For example, a school which only admitted white children would be directly discriminating. Direct discrimination is very rare in education nowadays.

Indirect discrimination is more common, more difficult to identify and can often be unintentional. It occurs when the same qualification is applied to everybody but is such that more people of one race or sex can comply with it. To be unlawful the condition imposed must be unjustifiable. An example would be if a school said that all students in woodwork classes had to be over 5'6" tall, since a great many more boys could comply than girls.

Discrimination on the grounds of either race or sex is specifically unlawful if it:

● applies to the terms on which a school offers to admit pupils

● is the reason for a refusal of an application for a child's admission

● it discriminates in the way benefits, facilities and services are offered

As regards sex discrimination, there are certain exceptions. These include single-sex schools, single-sex schools which are becoming co-educational, further education courses in physical training and some sporting activities where girls would be at a disadvantage because of their physical capacity.

Complaining about discrimination

If a child has been the victim of discrimination, a complaint has to be made on their behalf by their parent or guardian. The first step is usually to complain in writing to the Secretary of State for Education. If the complaint is not remedied within two months then another complaint should be made to the county court. Where the complaint is about sex discrimination the court will be the nearest county court. In cases involving racial discrimination only certain county courts can be used.

If the court finds the complaint proved it can:

● make a declaration setting out the rights of the parties

- make recommendations as to what action the school or LEA should take

- award damages. In cases of indirect discrimination it can only award damages if the discrimination was intentional.

Discrimination cases can be difficult to prove and it is advisable to get help from either the Commission for Racial Equality, the Equal Opportunities Commission, or the National Council for Civil Liberties.

Children with special educational needs

LEAs have a duty to make provision for children with special educational needs. They are also obliged to try to educate these children with the others, rather than sending them to special schools. Despite this many children with special educational needs are still educated in special schools, often privately.

The law says that a child should be considered to have special educational needs if the child has significantly greater difficulty in learning than the majority of children of his or her age, or has a disability preventing him or her making use of appropriate educational facilities. The law applies to children under five, as well as those of school age.

Assessing a child's needs

In order to ascertain the type of provision that should be made for a child with special needs, the LEA can carry out assessments. If the child is under two this can only be done with the parents' consent.

In all cases parents have to be told of proposed assessments and can make representations about them. Parents can also appeal to the Secretary of State if they disagree with the findings of such assessments. When making the assessment the LEA must receive written educational, psychological and medical reports.

At the end of the assessment the LEA will make a statement of the child's special educational needs. The proposals should be served on the child's parents together with the advice on which the LEA is basing its decision. Parents can make representations to the LEA about the statement and can ask for a meeting with an officer of the LEA to discuss the matter. Parents can appeal against the statement to a local appeal committee and, if necessary, beyond that to the Secretary of State.

Parents can request assessments but the LEA can refuse unless the child is under two. The LEA should not refuse an assessment unless it thinks it is unreasonable. Parents can request reassessment of their children and should do so if there has been a significant change in the child's circumstances or where it is more than six months from the last assessment. Assessments form the basis of the LEA's decision about the child's schooling and can restrict parents' rights to choose the child's school (see page 87).

Private schools

Parents can choose if they wish to send their children to fee-paying schools, many of which provide boarding places. Fee-paying schools are not run by LEAs but instead are privately owned. Although independent of the state system they have to be registered with the Department of Education and Science. The DES will register the school if it meets the minimum standards laid down for the standard of its premises, accommodation, staff and teaching. As long as a school meets the minimum standards it can organize itself as it chooses. There is a great deal of variation between schools.

Fees vary from school to school. Many schools, however, have scholarships which can pay all or part of the fees for some pupils. The government has also set up the assisted places scheme (see below) which can pay fees for some pupils at some schools.

School fees have to be paid out of taxed income although some tax relief is available for separated parents where the fees are paid under a school fees order (see page 36).

Further and higher education

LEAs must provide education for pupils up to the age of 19 if they request it. This is usually provided either in schools or colleges of further education.

Further education for degree, diploma courses and other qualifications is provided in polytechnics, usually run by LEAs, or in universities. Universities are self-governing institutions for which the Secretary of State has overall responsibility. The government assists universities with funding.

Grants

There are many grants available that can be made by local education authorities for educational purposes. Some must be offered and some are at the discretion of the LEA.

Grants the education authority must make

A student is entitled to be considered for a grant if he or she:

● is normally resident in the local education's area

● has the necessary educational qualifications and is attending a full-time course at a university, college or other institution in Great Britain or Northern Ireland

● is studying a first-degree course or a comparable course, or a course for a Diploma of Higher Education or the Higher National Diploma, or a course for teacher training or for a full-time course for Higher Diploma for the Technical Education Council or the Business Education Council

These powers and duties are subject to the ability of the authority to suspend or terminate awards in certain circumstances. In general, applications for the grant must reach the authority before the date the course is due to begin. Such grants are means-tested and the pupil and the parents' income will be taken into account.

Discretionary awards

In addition to the mandatory awards for courses of higher education there are also a number of courses for which many LEAs will give grants. The advice of the local authorities should be sought in such cases.

Assisted places at independent schools

The Secretary of State operates an assisted places scheme whereby pupils who might not otherwise benefit from education at independent schools can have their fees paid. The rules state that the child concerned must have lived in the United Kingdom, the Channel Islands or the Isle of Man for three years and must be over 11 years old. The school concerned selects from eligible pupils the children to be offered assisted places. The scheme only applies to certain schools who participate in the scheme.

Education benefits

LEAs have the power to make certain grants for school pupils for uniforms and maintenance. These are more fully dealt with in Chapter 9.

7 Employment

Until well into the nineteenth century children frequently worked long hours for low wages and in quite dreadful conditions. The industrial revolution, which led to the migration of large numbers to the North of England, resulted in widespread hardship among those employed in factories, mines and mills. Children became much-needed breadwinners in such families. Reforms were not easily obtained in the face of organized and powerful opposition from industrialists.

Gradually, however, changes were made. Successive laws reduced children's working hours, laid down minimum levels for education and forbade the employment of children in certain industries.

Ironically, today the major problem that many school leavers face is getting a job at all. If they do get work then it is likely to be poorly paid. Training is also widely considered to be inadequate. Most young people do not have the rights of other employees against unfair dismissal, to redundancy pay and maternity provision because they have not worked for employers long enough. Government training schemes—notably the Youth Training Scheme (YTS)—often offer no real hope of a job at the end.

School children and employment

Much of this chapter concentrates on the law that governs the employment of school children, that is, those children under 16. Contrary to popular belief many school children work and in a wide range of occupations.

Exact figures are not available but a study of 1,712 children in London and Luton in Bedfordshire, carried out by the

Low Pay Unit in 1982–83, produced some surprising results. It showed that 40 percent of all the children in the survey had jobs during term-time. This figure did not include those employed in babysitting, running errands and the like. A significant number of those employed were aged 11 and 12.

The range of work done was also very wide. The highest percentage (33 percent) worked delivering newspapers, followed by farming (13.6 percent), cleaning offices, hotels, and so on (12.8 percent), building construction and repair (6.6 percent), grocery, bakery and other food shops (6 percent) and pubs and off-licences (5.9 percent).

Much of this employment is illegal. Indeed, 83 percent of the children surveyed in London were working illegally.

Restrictions on the employment of children

As far as employment law is concerned, a child is defined as someone of compulsory school age, basically anyone between the ages of five and 16. The employment of children is subject to strict legal conditions, although these do not seem to be rigorously enforced. The law says that no child can be employed under the age of 13 years.

Children over 13 who are still under the compulsory school-leaving age can work part-time but not:

- during school hours on any day when school is open
- before 7 am or after 7 pm on any day
- for more than two hours on any day on which the child is required to attend school, or on a Sunday
- in any job where the child would be required to lift, carry or move anything heavy enough to be likely to cause injury to the child.

Employment is defined as assisting in a trade or occupation carried on for profit whether or not this work is paid. This definition excludes babysitting, odd jobs and gardening. There are also specific conditions attaching to certain types of employment.

Local authority restrictions

Local authorities can make local bye-laws to further restrict
children's employment. These should be available for inspection
at the town hall. These vary greatly from authority to authority
but they can, for example, completely forbid the employment
of children in any specified job.

They can further restrict the age below which children are not to
be employed and the number of hours in each day or week that
they can work. Bye-laws can also regulate the times to be allowed
for rest periods and meals, and specify the holidays to be allowed.
Local authorities can also make the employment of children
subject to a permit granted to the employer by the local education
authority and can demand that employers give them details of the
children they employ or propose to employ.

Local authority bye-laws cannot override the general restrictions
on the employment of children. They can, however, allow
children to be employed by their parents in light agricultural or
horticultural work while the children are under the age of 13 and
allow them to do that work for up to an hour before school.

Local education authorities also have the power to prohibit the
employment of a particular child who is registered as a pupil at a
state school or one maintained by the state, if it feels that to be
employed may harm the child's health or prevent the child getting
the best from his or her education. The education authority can
serve a written notice on the employer either stopping him from
employing the child or imposing such restrictions on the child's
employment as it feels necessary. An employer who disregards
such a notice can be prosecuted and fined and, in the last resort,
sentenced to a short term of imprisonment.

The Inner London Education Authority bye-laws provide an
example of what an authority can do. These bye-laws state, for
example, that no child can work in the mornings before school
unless delivering milk or newspapers. Under these bye-laws the
maximum a child can be employed in any week is five hours, which
is shorter than the government levels.

One difficulty with regulation through bye-laws is the wide
variation between authorities. In an attempt to rationalize this the
Employment of Children Act 1973 provided a model and uniform
set of bye-laws which would apply to all local

authorities. That Act is not in force, largely because of opposition from local authorities who felt that the cost of implementation would be too high. It does not seem likely that the law will be implemented in the near future.

Special employment restrictions

The following section deals with additional special regulations for certain kinds of occupation. This is not an exhaustive list and for other occupations the advice of the Local Education Authority or the Health and Safety Executive should be sought.

MINES AND QUARRIES

Women generally are not allowed to work in any job which would require them to spend a significant part of their working time in a mine below ground. This exception does not apply in the case of disused mines. This general restriction applies to girls as well as to women.

Boys under the age of 16 cannot be employed below ground at a mine except to receive instruction.

FACTORIES AND OTHER INDUSTRIAL UNDERTAKINGS

Special regulations restrict the employment of children and young people in factory work. The term 'factory' includes any premises in which people are employed in making, altering, repairing, decorating, finishing, washing, breaking up, demolishing or adapting anything for sale, slaughtering animals or holding animals awaiting slaughter. This definition covers many places not normally thought of as factories, for example, a hospital workshop used for the repair of hospital equipment.

Industrial undertakings include construction, electrical undertakings, and road, rail, transport, docks and demolition work.

The employment of a child under 16 in any industrial undertaking, including a factory, is prohibited. There is an exception to this for children employed in an industrial undertaking in which only members of his or her family are employed. Technical school training shops are also excluded.

The law also makes special regulations for people who are over 16 but under 18 years old. These limit the numbers of hours young people can work, lay down minimum rest periods and include restrictions on night work.

The law here is very muddled and almost certainly widely broken. There is a great need for the law to be clearly set out so that it can be at least understood. Enforcement is poor and penalties for employers, if they are prosecuted, low.

SHOPS

Rules also restrict the hours that young people can work in shops. Again the law is muddled and matters are made worse by the fact that some jobs could be defined both as shop jobs and as jobs in factories and industrial undertakings. The law also lays down minimum hours for meals, rest breaks and holidays.

STREET TRADING

No one under 17 years old can be employed in street trading. There are certain exceptions to this. Local authority bye-laws sometimes allow young people under the age of 17 to work for their parents.

No one under the age of 18 is allowed to be employed in street trading on Sundays.

ENTERTAINMENT

A child is not allowed to take part in certain performances unless a licence has been granted by the local authority. The types of performance are:

- any performance for which any charge is made

- any performance in licensed premises or in a club

- any broadcast performance

- any performance recorded for use in a broadcast or film to be shown in public including rehearsals.

A licence is also required for a child who has taken part in other performances for more than three days in the last six months. Performances arranged by a school or by the local authority, for which the child does not receive any payment other than expenses, do not require licences.

If a licence is needed and the child is under 14 years old it will only be granted in certain circumstances:

- for acting in a part that has to be played by a child of that age

- for dancing in a ballet which forms part of an entertainment consisting entirely of ballet or opera in a part that was to be played by a child of that age

- for a part that is wholly or mainly musical, if the entertainment is wholly or mainly musical or consists only of opera and ballet.

Before granting a licence, the local authority must be satisfied that the child is fit to undertake the performance and that proper provision has been made to ensure that the child's health and welfare are safeguarded and that his or her education will not suffer. An application for licence has to be made in writing on a form provided by the local authority. It must be signed by the person applying for the licence, the child's parent, and has to be accompanied by a number of other documents including two copies of a photograph of the child.

The granting of licences is also subject to a number of other requirements and advice should be sought from the local authority. The applicant for the licence can appeal to a magistrates' court against the refusal to grant one. It is an offence for anybody, including the child's parent, to allow a child to take part in any performance without complying with the law or to lie when applying for the licence.

There are special rules for dangerous performances. These include acrobatic performances and all performances as a contortionist. No child under 12 may be trained to take part in such performances and a licence is needed before anybody under the age of 16 can be trained.

A child under the age of 18 cannot go abroad to sing, play, perform or exhibit for profit unless a licence has been granted and this can be enforced by a place of safety order (see page 53). The restriction does not apply if the young person is only temporarily resident in the United Kingdom. Applications for licences for this kind of employment must be made to the magistrates' court.

MESSENGERS, DELIVERY BOYS AND GIRLS AND RELATED OCCUPATIONS

There are special provisions relating to the employment of people under 18 years old in: the collection and delivery of goods; carrying, loading or unloading of goods in hotels or clubs; carrying messages; running errands; public swimming baths, bathing places or Turkish baths; lift operation; operating cinematograph apparatus; laundries; dyeing and cleaning works; and places where intoxicating liquor may lawfully be sold or supplied after 11 pm.

A young person cannot work for more than 48 hours in any week in such employment. Where seasonal pressures make extra hours necessary a person over 16 can work overtime so long as that does not exceed six hours in any week or 50 in any year. Overtime can only be worked for 12 weeks in the year.

A young person cannot be employed continuously in such premises for more than five hours without a meal or rest interval of at least $\frac{1}{2}$ hour. If the working time covers the period from 11.30 am to 2.30 pm at least $\frac{3}{4}$ hour must be allowed for lunch. On at least one weekday the young person has to finish work by 1 pm and must be off work for a period of at least 11 consecutive hours in every 24 hours from midday to midday, including the period from 10 pm to 6 am.

A young person can only work on Sundays if a whole day's holiday is given on a weekday. This must not be the weekday on which the young person cannot be employed after 1 pm.

LICENSED PREMISES

Young people under 18 cannot be employed during opening hours in a bar or premises licensed to sell intoxicating liquor. This includes off-licences.

BETTING SHOPS

No one under 18 may be employed in a betting shop.

THE USE OF EQUIPMENT

There are specific regulations covering the use of equipment by children and young people. The main ones are:

● No one under 13 may drive or ride an agricultural tractor or machine.

● No one under 16 can operate a circular saw, handle poisonous substances, use equipment without proper safety precautions or clean machinery which may expose them to injury.

Employment rights

Many employees' rights depend on length of service. As a result most young people are excluded.

Unfair dismissal and redundancy

An employee is not entitled to make a claim against unfair dismissal or to claim redundancy pay unless they have worked continuously for the employer for over 16 hours per week for two years. Employees who work between eight and 16 hours a week cannot make a claim until they have worked for the employer for five years.

Maternity leave and maternity pay

To be eligible for maternity leave a woman must have worked for her employer for at least 16 hours per week for two years by the beginning of the eleventh week before the expected date of confinement; or for five years if she works between eight and 16 hours per week. The same conditions govern eligibility to maternity pay, although not maternity benefit.

Training

Most training in the United Kingdom is carried out by employers and is often of a very poor standard. Most professions, such as nursing, have special training programmes. Details of these should be available from schools and colleges and the professional organizations concerned.

Some employers provide day-release schemes enabling young people to attend college while they are working. Again the careers staff at school should be able to advise on this.

Apprenticeships

Apprenticeships are a form of training in the workplace. They are less common than they used to be and are mainly found in male-dominated jobs such as engineering. The big exception is hairdressing.

A contract of apprenticeship has to be in writing. It can be entered into by a young person under the age of 18, who will be bound by it if the contract is for his or her benefit (see page 112). Sometimes the employer will demand that a parent act as guarantor for a contract of apprenticeship in case the young person cancels the agreement on reaching 18. It is more difficult, though not impossible, to dismiss an apprentice than other types of employee. Apprentices are usually poorly paid.

Some contracts of apprenticeship require that the apprentice or his or her parent pay the employer a premium for taking the apprentice on. If the employer goes bankrupt before the apprenticeship has finished the apprentice can sometimes claim the premium back from the government.

Youth Training Scheme (YTS)

The Youth Training Scheme was introduced in 1983 with the aim of providing all 16-year-old school leavers with training opportunities. It is run by the Manpower Services Commission.

WHO IS ELIGIBLE?

Those eligible to take part in YTS are:

- all school leavers aged 16 and 17 who are not in work
- 18- to 21-year-old school leavers who are disabled
- some young people who are apprenticed
- young people who have completed a vocational training course
- 18 year olds who could not enter YTS earlier because of pregnancy, because they stayed on at school to learn English, or because they were serving custodial sentences

YTS COURSES

Courses run for two years for 16 year olds and for one year for 17 year olds. They consist of a mixture of work and off-the-job education and training. Eighteen year olds who could not start earlier can also receive two years' training, as can disabled young people.

Some courses are organized by local authorities and some by private employers. All courses, however, must consist of a minimum of off-the-job training. This is 20 weeks for a two-year YTS and seven weeks for a one-year YTS. All trainees now get a training agreement spelling out their rights and responsibilities and giving details of pay, holidays and so on. It is not legally binding. At the end of training, a certificate is given. There is no guaranteed job at the end of YTS.

PAY

Currently, weekly allowance of £27.30 is paid to all two-year YTS trainees in the first year of training, which goes up to £35.00 in the second year. Those on a year programme receive £27.30 for the first 13 weeks and £35.00 per week for the remaining nine months. Trainees are repaid travelling expenses of over £3.00 per week. A lodging allowance can also be paid where the training takes place away from home.

YTS trainees who have a family or dependants living with them may be eligible for Supplementary Benefit. Normally, however, a single person will find that their income from YTS is higher than Supplementary Benefit levels and will not be able to claim.

CONDITIONS OF WORK

The government has laid down some conditions of employment for those on YTS. Trainees must:

● usually not be made to work more than 40 hours per week. Overtime is not allowed.

● be given up to three weeks paid sick leave before losing their allowance.

● be given at least 18 days and not more than 20 days holiday per year.

The government has not given full rights under the sex and race discrimination legislation to YTS trainees. Nor are all the provisions of the health and safety legislation applicable to all trainees.

Property and Contracts

Money and other property

From birth children are entitled to own money and property, with the exception of land (see page 110). Normally, when a child is very young, property must be administered either by trustees, or by the child's parents. The property still belongs to the child and the trustees must administer it for the child's benefit. Sometimes children are left money on trust. This, too, will be administered by trustees until the child becomes entitled to it.

Bank accounts

Children of any age can open accounts at most banks although practice varies. Bank accounts are frequently opened for children but the banks usually do not allow a child to withdraw money until the child is old enough to understand the nature of the transaction. In the case of National Savings Banks and Trustee Savings Banks children cannot open accounts until they are seven, at which time they can withdraw money from the account as well as pay money in. A young person under the age of 18 cannot open a Post Office Giro Bank account without the signature of a parent or guardian.

Generally banks will not allow people under 18 overdrafts because of the difficulty in enforcing the repayment of debts (see page 111). The same applies to granting children credit.

Business interest

Children under 18 can be partners in trades and businesses but they are not liable for the firm's debts or the actions of their co-partners. These conditions make them a fairly unattractive proposition for most partnerships.

Children's earnings

Children's earnings are their own property. It is not clear whether parents are entitled to deduct a reasonable amount for the child's upkeep.

Land and real property

Children under the age of 18 cannot legally own land and real property. This includes houses, flats and other buildings, as well as land itself. A child who is entitled to an interest in land and property will usually have to have it administered by trustees.

Trustees can pay all or part of the income from the property to the child's parents or guardians for the child's upkeep. Trustees can decide whether or not they do this and must take account of the child's needs and any other income available. Trustees can sometimes make advances of capital as well, although the law here is complex.

Inheritance

If a parent dies intestate, that is without making a will, their spouse will inherit the first £40,000 of the estate and all personal goods. The remainder will be inherited by the children, although the surviving parents will have what is known as a 'life interest' in half of it. This means, for example, that if the property produces an income the parent will be entitled to half of it. If there is no surviving parent, the children inherit the whole estate. This includes any illegitimate children.

Property left to children in a will includes illegitimate children unless the will specifies otherwise.

Money or personal property left to a child under 18 in a will can present difficulties. The executor of the will may be liable to the child if he pays the money to the child or his/her parents.

Children can apply to the court if their parents have made no provision, or insufficient provision, for them in their will. This covers legitimate and illegitimate children as well as an unborn child.

The court has wide powers to make maintenance payments and awards out of the dead person's estate. In deciding what, if any, order to make the court has to decide whether the will made reasonable provision for the child. It then has to consider the financial needs and resources of those applying as well as those of the beneficiaries. Such applications are complicated and legal advice should be sought.

Contracts

Children, that is anyone under 18 years old, are not considered fully liable for the consequences of their actions when it comes to making agreements, and cannot usually be bound by them. The restriction operates to protect the child and not the other party to the agreement. A child can always sue for breach of a contract.

This restriction does not usually matter as the agreements that children usually enter into usually concern very small amounts of money and no harm is done if the child changes his or her mind, for example when buying sweets in a sweetshop. However, things could be more serious if, for example, a child agrees to buy an expensive tropical fish and a petshop owner had to order one specially. If the child then decided not to buy the fish the owner would have no redress against the child. If the child's parents had been involved in the transaction the position would be different (see page 112 below).

There are a few exceptions to this rule. In certain cases a child can be bound by contracts they have entered into.

Contracts for necessaries

The theory behind the law is that it is desirable for a child to be able to pay for and be bound by an agreement to purchase items that are necessary or constitute the necessities of life. Necessaries are defined as 'goods suitable to the conditions in life of the minor and to his actual requirements at the time of sale or delivery'. What is included in this definition is not specified but this does not in practice seem to cause many problems.

'Necessaries' have been held to include food, clothing, medicine, rent, funeral expenses for a member of the child's family, educational expenses, military uniforms, engagement and wedding rings, and gifts to fiances. If a young person has a moped and needs insurance, this would be a contract for necessaries.

Such definitions, however, only go so far to making the situation clear. In any action taken against a young person to enforce a debt, the person taking the action has to show not only that the goods concerned were necessaries, but also that they were needed by the young person at the time, and that the young person would not otherwise have them or have enough of them.

The practical consequences of what seems a rather old-fashioned part of the law are difficult to predict. For example, a young person who joins the army will be provided with a uniform and will usually have to sign an agreement that if he leaves the army he will have to repay the cost of the uniform. Because the uniform has been held to be necessary he will be bound by the agreement even though he entered into it under the age of 18. Likewise, if goods are sent to young people they may keep them without paying unless the goods are necessaries. The same applies to goods bought on credit. However, because of these restrictions credit is rarely offered to people under 18.

Contracts of employment and apprenticeship

People under 18 can enter into binding contracts of employment or apprenticeship. Indeed, most contracts of apprenticeship are entered into by people who are under 18. Such contracts are enforceable, both against and by the young person, if they are for the young person's benefit. An agreement, for example, between a young performer or musician and his or her manager would be enforceable even if the young person was under 18.

Contractual liability of parents and other adults

If an adult is party to an agreement with a child which can only be carried out by the adult and the child together, the contract cannot be enforced unless it comes within the exceptions outlined above. However, where the contract could be performed by the adult alone, then even though it cannot be enforced against the child it can be enforced against the adult.

Other civil actions

Children's liability

A child can be sued for the consequences of damage he or she causes. There are special rules relating to the way in which the action can be brought (see page 114). These rules mean that if someone is injured as a result of a child's negligence, or damage is caused because of a child's action or by a child's animal, or by the child trespassing on other people's property then the child can be sued. A child can also be sued for the return of money he or she steals.

Children cannot be sued if they are too young to understand the difference between right and wrong. A child cannot be sued if the loss is due to a contract for which the child could not be sued.

Parents' liability

Parents can be liable for damage caused by their children if the child is in their control. If parents are negligent in looking after a child, for example by allowing a child to use something which is dangerous or by not exercising proper control and supervision, they may be liable. Parents may also be liable if they have specifically authorized the child to do the act which caused the damage. Parents can also be liable for injuries suffered by a third person arising from a dangerous situation created by the innocent act of a child.

Others' liability

In the same way that parents can be liable for the negligent acts of children, so can teachers when the child is at school or under their control. When the child is in care, local authorities, or indeed anybody else who lawfully has the care of the child, may be liable. In the case of a child who left a children's home and burned down the local church the local authority was liable for the damage caused.

Legal actions concerning children

It is not unusual for circumstances to arise in which a child can sue or be sued. For example, if a child is run over and suffers injury the child may be entitled to damages. In the same way, if a child causes an injury, for example, by causing a car to swerve the child may be liable.

The law says that a child under 18 cannot sue in his or her own name. Instead, the court case has to be brought by an adult on the child's behalf. This will usually be a child's parent but might need to be someone else if the child's interests conflicted with those of a parent, which can sometimes happen. If the child is in the care of the local authority, the action will have to be brought by the local authority on behalf of the child.

The person who brings the action is called the child's 'next friend'. The child's next friend must legally employ a solicitor. If there is nobody else available to act as the child's next friend then the Official Solicitor can do so (see page 12). The next friend can apply for legal aid on the child's behalf (see page 13).

A person who acts as a child's next friend for the purposes of taking court proceedings can make themselves liable in two ways. Firstly, if the child loses the case and the court orders the child to pay costs it is the child's next friend who is legally liable for these. If, however, the child has legal aid, in practice, the court will not usually award costs against the child.

The other way in which the next friend can be liable is by settling the case but for a lower amount than the child could expect to get. In those circumstances the child could sue the next friend when he or she reaches the age of 18. It is not possible to settle a case involving a child after the proceedings have begun without it being approved by the court. If the settlement is approved by the court the child will lose the right to sue. In any event, even if proceedings have not been started the next friend can ask the court to approve any settlement.

TIME LIMITS FOR CHILDREN SUING

There are time limits laid down by law for beginning court actions. Generally, if a person is injured as a result of someone else's negligence or carelessness the action has to be brought within three years of the date of the accident. For breaches of contract, the action has to be started within six years of the breaking of the agreement. For cases involving children, however, these periods of time do not begin to run until the child reaches his or her eighteenth birthday. This right is designed to protect children whose parents do not pursue action on their behalf.

This does not prevent the action being started earlier. In fact, it is advisable to do so as it will mean that the court case can take place when the events are fresh in everybody's mind.

Benefits

The state benefit system in Britain is extremely complicated. This section will concentrate on benefits which concern children or relate to them and, in particular, to benefits which children can claim.

The whole system of state benefits is under review at the present time. Wherever possible proposed changes to individual benefits have been included. It must be remembered, however, that these changes are only proposals and may alter at a later date.

The benefits system

Benefits fall into two major categories: those which are means-tested and those which are not.

Means-tested benefits

A means-tested benefit is one where the income and capital of the person claiming the benefit is taken into account when assessing their entitlement and the amount of benefit. Means-tested benefits which most affect children are supplementary benefits, family income supplement, health and education benefits.

Non-means-tested benefits

Non-means-tested benefits do not depend on the income and capital resources of the person claiming them but are available so long as the claimant meets other conditions. Non-means-tested benefits themselves fall into two categories: contributory benefits and non-contributory benefits.

To be eligible for a contributory benefit the claimant must not only meet the other conditions for eligibility but must also have been paid or been credited with the appropriate number of National Insurance contributions. Non-contributory benefits do not depend on National Insurance contributions having been paid.

The most important contributory benefit affecting children and young people is unemployment benefit. Young people should bear in mind that contributions are important in later years in order to establish eligibility for pensions, maternity allowances and sickness benefit as well as other benefits.

Non-contributory benefits which do not depend on National Insurance contributions and which are of particular importance to children are child benefit and some benefits payable to disabled people.

National Insurance contributions

There are four different types of contribution. The most important class of contribution is Class I, which is payable by all employed earners and their employers and gives, as long as the appropriate levels of contributions have been paid, an entitlement to all contributory non-means-tested benefits.

Liability to pay National Insurance contributions starts at the school-leaving age of 16 and lasts throughout a person's working life, that is, to age 60 for women and age 65 for men. Class I contributions become payable where a person's earnings are above a minimum level and rise on a scale up to a maximum limit. The earnings level below which contributions are not payable for 1985–86 is currently £35.50 per week. The upper limit beyond which no additional contributions are payable is £265 per week. Contributions are payable by both the employee and the employer and are calculated as a percentage of the person's earnings. The percentage goes up in bands so that a higher percentage is paid at the top level of earnings than at the bottom end. The percentage also varies depending on whether employees are part of the state earnings related pension scheme (SERPS).

An important feature of the National Insurance contribution scheme is that people who are studying or otherwise unemployed can be given credits. This means that they will be credited with having made a contribution without actually paying it. Most importantly, credits are given to young people up to the age of 18 who are not earning. Training and education credits are given for those in further education as long as they started their course before they were 21.

Training credits are also available for young people who are undertaking an approved training course. All courses run by the Manpower Services Commission will count. The courses have to be of a vocational, technical or similar nature. In order to qualify the young person has to be over 18 at the beginning of the National Insurance contribution year and the course must last for less than a year. Certain other National Insurance contribution requirements also have to be met.

The Department of Health and Social Security (DHSS)

The DHSS is responsible for administering the benefits system in the United Kingdom. The nearest office can be found by looking up Health and Social Security in the telephone book. A person who has queries about benefit is best advised to visit or write to the office rather than telephone. It is also a good idea to keep copies of all correspondence with the department.

The department is not noted for its helpfulness and young people who encounter problems should seek assistance from a specialist organization. Citizens' Advice Bureaux will often give advice and deal with the department on behalf of a claimant. Other organizations who can help are listed at the end of this book.

Emergencies

If an emergency occurs out of office hours, emergency payments of supplementary benefit can be made. Each local office has a member of staff on duty at the weekends. They can be contacted by telephoning the office. In London there is a special emergency office (Address: DHSS, Keyworthy House, Keyworthy Street, London SE1. Telephone: 01–928–8077 or 01–407–2315).

Supplementary benefit

Supplementary benefit is sometimes described as the safety net of the welfare state. It is paid to people whose resources are below a level set by the government and who meet a number of other conditions.

Claimants must not be in full-time work. This is normally 30 hours or more a week. People who are physically or mentally disabled or on government training schemes may be considered to be not in full-time work even if they are working more than 30 hours a week.

Claimants have to sign on to show that they are available for full-time work. Exceptions to this condition include those who are pregnant, are incapable of working because of illness or a disability, people on government training schemes and some students (see below). Anyone claiming supplementary benefit has to show that their income and capital fall below levels laid down by the DHSS. Capital under £5,000 is ignored. Over that amount a person is not entitled to claim supplementary benefit. Income has to be below the supplementary benefit rates.

Claiming is not as simple as it sounds. In calculating income, for example, some benefits are not counted at all, some are counted in full and others in part. If in doubt advice should be sought. Young people cannot claim supplementary benefit in their own right until they are over 16.

Rates

At the time of writing, the rates at which supplementary benefit is paid are:

	Basic rate
Husband and wife	£48.40
Single householder	£29.80
Any other person aged	
18 or over	£23.85
16–17 years	£18.40
11–15 years	£15.30
0–10 years	£10.20

Higher rates can be paid in certain circumstances where the person has been claiming for a long period of time. Lower rates apply where a family or claimant is living in a hostel or board-and-lodging accommodation. For more about board and lodging accommodation see page 132.

Children under 16

An adult claiming supplementary benefit who has a child under 16 living with them can claim supplementary benefit for the child as a dependant. The child does not have to be the claimant's child.

Supplementary benefit is not payable for children who are living with foster parents on an official basis. If the fostering arrangement has been made privately, the foster parent can claim supplementary benefit, although any payment that the foster parent receives from the child's own parents would have to be disclosed to the DHSS and would be treated as part of their resources.

Young people over 16

Young people over 16 can claim supplementary benefit in their own right if they meet the other requirements the law lays down. The entitlement rules for supplementary benefit are complex but the ones most likely to affect young people are:

- that they are unemployed
- that their capital and income are less than supplementary benefit limits
- and that they sign on for work

Young people who are living with their parents and claiming benefit will probably be treated as 'non-householders' and will receive £18.40 per week when 16 or 17 years old and £23.85 per week thereafter. A higher long-term rate can be paid to young people who are either disabled, or who have not been required to sign on for work for 12 months.

School leavers

A young person who has left school or college will not usually be able to claim benefit until the beginning of the next term and will be treated as a dependant in the household in which they are living. This means that a young person leaving school at Christmas will not be able to claim until the first Monday in January. One who leaves at Easter cannot claim until the first Monday after Easter Monday and those who leave school in June cannot claim until the first Monday in September.

A student who leaves but returns to school or college simply to take exams will be treated as having left school as long as the total time spent in taking exams is less than 12 hours.

Students under 19

Students who are under 19 and receiving what is called 'relevant education' cannot normally apply for supplementary benefit. There are exceptions to this. Parents of a student under 19 who is living at home and who are in receipt of supplementary benefit can claim benefit for their child as a dependant.

A student will be treated as being in relevant education if the course is a non-advanced one, that is, up to and including A levels or the Scottish Certificate of Education at Higher Level and lasts more than 12 hours a week excluding homework and meal breaks. A student whose course lasts for 12 hours a week or less can claim benefit but will have to be available for work.

Students who are over 16 and in relevant education can sometimes claim benefit, without having to sign on, if they are:

- a parent and their child is living with them

- so handicapped that it is unlikely that he or she would get a job in the next 12 months

- an orphan and has no one acting as their parent

- living away from his or her parents or people who are acting in the place of parents, or is estranged from them. A young person in local authority care is treated as living with people acting in the place of parents so would not be able to fall within this provision. Young people should be treated as being estranged if they have no intention or wish to live with their parents or any substitute and no wish to have any prolonged physical or emotional association with them.

Students over 19 on full-time courses

A course is normally counted as full-time if the college or university says it is. This decision is not final and can be challenged by the DHSS. Supplementary benefit is not normally payable for students over 19 years old but there are exceptions:

● If the student is living with parents or with other people who are claiming benefit, those people can claim benefit for the young person as a dependant, although any grant received will have to be taken into account.

● If the young person is undergoing secondary education, has done so for the last two years and became 19 on or after the first day of the autumn term, he or she can claim. This covers young people who have stayed on at school.

● Students on full-time courses can get benefit if they are single parents, or they are disabled and would be unlikely to get a job within a reasonable period of time compared to other students, or if they live with an unmarried partner who is not a student and who has been ill for the last eight weeks.

Students over 19 on part-time courses

Students on part-time courses will usually only be able to claim benefit if the course lasts 21 hours or less a week, not counting meal breaks and unsupervised study. The young person must be prepared to give up the course immediately a suitable job comes up.

Single payments

A person on supplementary benefit can sometimes claim an extra allowance on top of their benefit. These are called 'single payments'. An application has to be made for each single payment.

Single payments are available for household expenses such as clothing, bedding and furniture. Many items, however, are excluded. These include: car expenses, telephone, television and radio costs, education or training needs, school uniforms, sports clothing or equipment, travelling expenses to and from school, school meals and meals during school holidays.

For many items for which claims can be made there is a fixed amount that can be given. Where no amount is specified the DHSS should give the claimant enough to buy something of reasonable quality.

A claimant has the right to appeal to a Supplementary Benefit Appeal Tribunal against the refusal of a special payment. To lodge the appeal the claimant should write to the DHSS officer dealing with the claim within 28 days of receiving the reasons for the refusal.

Proposed changes

The government proposes to change supplementary benefit to a new benefit called 'income support'. This will be paid at a basic rate with special additions for certain categories of people including those with disabilities and single parents. There will also be a family premium for claimants who have dependant children living with them. Most importantly, people under 25 will be paid at a lower rate.

A social fund will be set up and each local office will be responsible for administering their part of it. Expenses that are now met by single payments will be paid for out of the social fund. Only a fixed amount of social fund money will be made available to each local office every year and, if that runs out, the office will not be able to make any more payments.

Child benefit

Child benefit cannot be claimed by a child but is paid to those who have responsibility for a child under 16, or a child between 16 and 19 receiving full-time education.

The person claiming has to be responsible for the child and this usually means that the child must be living with them. There are exceptions to this. If a child is away from home for up to 56 days in 16 weeks the absence will be ignored. This covers children of separated parents who go to stay with the other parent and also means that parents whose children have been taken into care will be entitled to claim child benefit for the first eight weeks.

In most cases the child must be resident in Great Britain. There
are exceptions for a child who is educated abroad. Holidays abroad
will not count unless they are very long. Normally the person
claiming child benefit will also have to live in Britain although
there are exceptions which cover short absences abroad and
members of the armed forces.

Children are not eligible if:

● they are married

● they are in care, prison or another form of custody, except for
   the first eight weeks

● they are entitled to a severe disablement allowance (see page
   132).

Forms for claiming child benefit are available from the DHSS.
When completed they should be sent to the Child Benefit Centre,
PO Box 1, Newcastle upon Tyne, NE88 1EA. Claims can be made
56 days before a baby is due and can be backdated for up to a
year.

Rates

Child benefit is currently payable at the rate of £7 per week per
child plus a single additional payment of £4.55 per week to single
parents. A parent will not be counted as a single parent if she is
living with her husband or the child's father or with someone else
as man and wife.

Family income supplement

Family income supplement is a benefit designed to help families
on low incomes. A family who qualifies will have their income
topped up to a level laid down by the government as being the
prescribed income level for a family of that size. People claiming
FIS are automatically entitled to other benefits, particularly health
benefits and free school meals.

Anybody can claim as long as they have one dependant child and
are in full-time work. Full-time work is defined as normally
working for 30 hours or more each week, except in the case of

single parents when it is defined as working 24 hours or more each week. If the family unit consists of a couple, FIS can be claimed by either of them if one is in full-time work.

Calculating FIS

When calculating FIS the DHSS start by looking at the gross earnings of the claimant and those of his or her partner, if any. Any income from lodgers is counted as well, although an allowance is made for expenses. Income of any dependant children is ignored except for any payments made to them for maintenance. Other types of income are also ignored, including child benefit, fostering allowances, attendance and mobility allowances and housing benefits. Once the department has calculated the amount of the gross income level it will be compared to the prescribed income level which varies according to the number of children in the family. If there is one child in the family the prescribed income limits are as follows:

Under 11	£97.50 per week
11–15	£98.50 per week
16 plus	£99.50 per week

For each additional child under 11 an additional £11.50 will be added. For each additional child between 11 and 15 an extra £12.50 will be added and for each additional child aged 16 and over £13.50 will be added.

The amount of FIS payable is calculated by subtracting the gross income from the prescribed level. The difference is the amount of FIS. Once the rate has been decided it lasts for 52 weeks regardless of whether people's circumstances change.

How to claim

Claims are made on Form FIS 1 obtainable from any post office or DHSS office. When completed they should be sent to DHSS (FIS), Poulton le Fylde, Blackpool, FY6 8WW.

Proposed changes

Under the government's new proposals family income supplement is to be replaced by a benefit called 'family credit'. It seems as though this will be calculated in much the same way as family income supplement but it will be added to the claimant's pay packet rather than paid separately through the DHSS. The benefit will be available to all people who work more than 24 hours a week instead of 30 hours a week and it will be assessed every six months instead of every year. The automatic entitlement to other benefits such as free school meals will go.

Health benefits

Free prescriptions

Children under 16 do not have to pay for prescriptions. Nor do children or young people over 16 if they are claiming supplementary benefit or family income supplement, or are dependants of people who are claiming these benefits or who are on low incomes. Many young people in work may also be entitled to free prescriptions since their wages are often low. To qualify a person's net income must not be more than £3.50 above supplementary benefit level. People who just miss qualifying for free prescriptions on the grounds of low income may still be able to claim a refund if they need more than one item because an extra £2 is added to the income level for each additional item prescribed.

Dental treatment, dentures and glasses

Young people under 18 and those who are under 19 who are at school, college or university full-time are entitled to free dental treatment. Dentures are free for children under 16 and those under 19 who are at school, college or university. Glasses are free for young people under 19 who are still at school, college or university.

Where a family is in receipt of supplementary benefit or FIS the whole family qualifies for free dental treatment, dentures or glasses. People on low incomes can also get exemptions entitling them to free dental treatment, dentures and glasses if their net income is not more than £2.50 above supplementary benefit level.

Those whose incomes are too high for free dental or optical treatment may sometimes only have to pay a reduced charge. The dentist or optician should be able to advise about this.

Free milk and vitamins

Children at a day nursery, playgroup or with a childminder can get one-third of a pint of milk for each day that they attend. The day nursery and the childminder have to be approved by the local authority and it is the childminder or playleader who has to apply. Handicapped children can get free milk if they are between five and 16 years old and not registered at a school or special school.

Low-income families, and families on supplementary benefit or claiming FIS, can also obtain free milk and vitamins for children up to the age of five years and one month, or longer if the child hasn't yet started school.

Fares to hospital

Costs of fares to and from hospital can be claimed by patients receiving supplementary benefit or FIS, or patients whose net income will be the same or lower than supplementary benefit once they have paid the fare. The amount covers the cost of the cheapest form of travel available.

Education benefits

School meals

Provision varies from authority to authority. The local education authority, however, has to make such provision as appears to be necessary for children whose parents receive supplementary benefit or family income supplement.

Uniform grants

Local authorities can make grants towards the cost of school uniform and other necessary clothing. Local authorities vary in their approach to this. In order to find out what provision is available, the local authority will have to be consulted. Since local authorities usually have a specific budget for these items which can run out quickly, claims should be made as early as possible in the school year.

Grants are not only given for school uniform but can be given for clothing or footwear needed for school and for sports equipment. Remember that school uniform expenses cannot be claimed as a single payment on supplementary benefit.

Educational maintenance allowances

These are discretionary awards which are payable to the parents of children who stay on at school after the school-leaving age of 16. They are paid by the local education authority. There is considerable variation but information will be available from the local education authority.

Fares to school

Where the child's home is more than two miles walking distance away from school for children under eight, or more than three miles away for older children, the local education authority has a duty to make arrangements for school transport. If special transport is not provided then the child's fares should be paid by the local education authority.

It has recently been held that in calculating the distance from the child's home to school the local education authority cannot exclude a child where a shorter journey would be difficult or dangerous, for example, through a wood.

Guardian's allowance

Guardian's allowance is paid to those looking after children who are, for all practicable purposes, orphans. It is a non-contributory benefit.

At present the guardian's allowance is £8.05 per week in respect of each child. It is non-taxable but if the person claiming it is claiming supplementary benefit it will be treated as part of their income.

In order to qualify the child must be living with the person claiming, who must also be entitled to child benefit (see page 123). The child for whom the payment is claimed will only qualify if:

- both parents have died

- one parent has died and the whereabouts of the other parent are unknown, and were unknown at the time of the death of the other parent. The department will expect to see evidence that the person claiming has tried to find the missing parent.

- one of the child's parents is dead and the other is serving a prison sentence of five years or more. Any part of the sentence which was served before the first parent died is discounted.

Step-parents do not count as parents for these purposes and so long as they meet the other conditions may be entitled to a guardian's allowance. In the case of an illegitimate child the mother only counts as the parent as long as the child's paternity has not been clearly established or admitted by the father.

In order to claim, at least one of the child's parents must have been born in the United Kingdom. There are also some residence requirements for the parents but these can be relaxed.

Benefits for disabled people

Attendance allowances

The attendance allowance is a non-contributory non-means-tested benefit. A person who meets the qualifying conditions can claim regardless of their income and capital and their National Insurance contributions.

At present the allowance is payable at two rates—£30.95 and £20.65 per week. The higher rate is generally payable if the person concerned needs 24-hour attendance. The main condition is that the person is so severely disabled, either physically or mentally, that he or she needs frequent assistance with bodily functions or continual supervision in order to avoid substantial danger to himself or others.

The allowance can be claimed for anybody over two years old. Where it is claimed for a child under 16 the claimant must show that the child requires supervision which is substantially greater than that normally required by a child of the same age or sex.

The attendance allowance for a child is paid to the person with whom the child is living. This can include people other than the parents. If the child goes into local authority care for example, to give the parents a break, or into hospital, the attendance allowance will cease after four weeks.

If a child is living permanently in care or stays most of the time in hospital but returns home temporarily, attendance allowance can be paid for each day that the child is at home.

Mobility allowance

Mobility allowance is paid to someone who has a physical disablement that renders them unable or virtually unable to walk and whose condition is likely to last for at least a year after the claim is made. It cannot be claimed for a child under five years old. At present mobility allowance is payable at a weekly rate of £21.65.

The disability must be physical. There have been difficulties with illnesses such as Down's Syndrome, although it does appear that the DHSS now usually accept that Down's Syndrome is a physical disability. People who suffer from disabilities which sometimes render them unable to walk are not generally able to claim mobility allowance. Claiming mobility allowance is often difficult and in such cases advice should be sought.

Invalid care allowance

Invalid care allowance is only payable to those over 16 years old. It is paid to a person who regularly cares for someone who receives an attendance allowance and who is not employed or in full-time education.

It can be claimed by someone who is looking after a child. In order to claim the attendance must be every day of the week and for a total of 35 hours a week. Temporary breaks will not lead to the loss of benefit if they are not longer than four weeks in any period of six months.

Invalid care allowances will stop if the patient is in hospital for more than four weeks at a time because his or her attendance allowance will stop at that point.

Married women and women who are cohabiting with a man are not at present entitled to claim the invalid care allowance. This is being challenged in a case being brought to the European Court of Justice.

Vaccine damage payments

Vaccine damage payments are lump sum payments of £20,000, payable to people who are severely disabled as a result of vaccination.

The vaccination must have been for diphtheria, tetanus, whooping cough, polio, measles, rubella (German measles) tuberculosis or smallpox. The vaccination must have been carried out in Britain or the Isle of Man after 5 July 1948, and, in the case of smallpox, before 1 August 1971. It must also have been administered when the person concerned was under 18 years old, unless the vaccination was for polio or rubella.

The person claiming must be at least two years old. If they have died the claim can be made by their next-of-kin but the child must have been at least two years old at the time of death, and death must have occurred after 9 May 1978.

Claims are made on a form available from the Vaccine Damage Payments Unit, DHSS, North Fylde, Central Offices, Norcross, Blackpool, FY5 3TA. It has to be made within six years of the vaccination or by the time the person is eight years old.

It is up to the Secretary of State to decide whether a person is entitled to a vaccine damage payment. The payment will be made only if the disability is sufficient and it can be shown that the vaccination was the cause of the disability.

Visits to handicapped children

The local education authority can meet all or part of the parent's fares to visit a child who is boarded away from home in order to receive special education and where the parent could not afford to visit the child otherwise.

Fares to children in care

Local authorities can pay for the parents to visit their children in care.

Death grants

Death grants are intended to be a payment towards the cost of funerals but do not have to be used for that purpose. The death grant is absurdly low and goes very little way towards meeting the typical cost of a funeral. It is paid at different rates according to the age of the person who dies. At present it is £30 for an adult, £22.50 for a child between the age of six and 18, £15 for a child between three and six and £9 for a child under three, unless the person was over 55 if a man, or over 50 if a woman on 5 July 1984 when the grant is £15.

Proposed changes

The death grant is to be abolished. Financial assistance for those on low incomes or pensions will be available from the social fund. This will be in the form of a loan which will have to be paid back either from the dead person's estate or from the resources of the person who claims the assistance.

Severe disablement allowance

This benefit cannot be claimed by those under 16 years old or under 19 if they are in full-time education. The conditions for entitlement are complex and advice should be sought.

At present the benefit is payable at the rate of £21.50 for the person claiming, with an additional £12.50 per week for an adult dependant and £7.65 per week for each dependant child.

Board and lodging allowances

Young people under 26 years old who are claiming supplementary benefit and living in lodgings can lose their entitlement to a board and lodging allowance in certain circumstances and may be required to move to another area before being eligible to claim it again. The law here is complicated and at the time of writing is subject to challenge in the courts. Advice should be sought from one of the organisations listed at the end of the book or from Citizens Advice Bureaux.

Official Documents

Registering a child's birth

A child must be registered within 42 days of birth. It is an offence not to register a birth. Special provisions can be made for registering a birth after 42 days.

Registration is free and is usually done at the local Registry of Births, Deaths and Marriages in the district where the child was born. The address of the local registrar should be available at the town hall or can be found in the telephone book under Registration of Births, Deaths and Marriages. In some areas registrars regularly visit local hospitals and will register the child's birth there.

Registration gives a record of a date and place of the child's birth and establishes a number of the child's civil rights such as entitlement to welfare services. It can often be an important document in questions concerning the child's citizenship or nationality (see Chapter 11).

Who can register the birth?

MARRIED PARENTS

If the child's parents are married, both parents have responsibility for registering the child's birth.

UNMARRIED PARENTS

In the case of an illegitimate child the mother has the responsibility for registering the birth. The father does not. The father of an illegitimate child cannot register the birth on his own but can register the birth together with the mother. Special provisions exist if the mother subsequently marries the child's father (see page 136).

OTHERS

If the parents are unable to register the birth anyone present at the birth or who has care of the child may do so. For example, if the parents die before the birth has been registered and a relative is looking after the child then they should register the birth.

Information required by the registrar

It is an offence for anybody to give false particulars when registering a birth. The registrar will wish to know:

● the date and place of the child's birth and, in the case of twins, the time

● the mother's name, surname, place of birth, usual address if this is different from the child's place of birth, and, if she is married, her maiden name

● the child's sex and name. The birth can be registered without the child being given a Christian name and then subsequently registered with the name as long as this is done within one year of the child's birth

● the name, surname, place of birth and occupation of the father, if the parents are married.

If the person who registers the birth is not the child's mother or father the registrar will also wish to know the name, surname, qualification and usual address of that person.

UNMARRIED PARENTS

If the parents are unmarried the father's name cannot be put on the birth certificate unless the mother and father both request it. In this case they must both sign the register.

The father's name can also be included if the mother requests it and can produce a statutory declaration signed by the father stating that he is the father and a declaration by her also saying that he is, or a certified copy of an affiliation order naming the father.

Birth certificates

Once the child's birth is registered a birth certificate is issued. This is free. There are two types of birth certificate—a long form and a short form. The person registering the birth can choose which they want. The short form of birth certificate leaves out details of the child's parents and so conceals the fact that a child is illegitimate.

Both forms of birth certificate are valid although a full birth certificate will be needed for some purposes. If the child is subsequently adopted, the court will need to see a copy of the full birth certificate, it will also be needed in any questions concerning the child's nationality. Adopted children receive a new birth certificate on their adoption.

Additional certified copies can be obtained for a fee, currently £5. They can be obtained from the place where the child's birth was registered, or from the Registrar General of Births, Deaths and Marriages, St Katherines House, Kingsway, London WC2. It takes about a year for entries from district registries to get to the Registrar General's office. If a copy of a birth certificate is required before that time it may only be available from the district registry where the birth was registered. Extra copies of adopted children's birth certificates are available from a different office (see page 196).

The child's name

It is up to the parents or the mother, in the case of an illegitimate child, to choose the child's name. There are no rules about what surname the child should take although it is still usual for children of married parents to be given the surname of their father.

There is no restriction on what names the child is given and the registrar must accept the parents' choice however ludicrous this is. However, the name does have to be registered in the English alphabet. If a child is given a Chinese name, for example, it will have to be registered in an English alphabetical translation and not in Chinese characters. A letter or a number can be included, such as George 3 Jones or Ann V James, but sequential numbers cannot. Any number of names can be chosen.

If the parents are not married the mother will normally give the child her own surname or the name of the father. The father does not have to consent to this but merely giving the child his surname is not evidence that the man is the child's father, in, say, affiliation proceedings (see page 37).

Re-registering of births

If the parents of an illegitimate child marry

If the mother of an illegitimate child marries the child's father within 12 months of the child's birth, the birth can be re-registered to name the child's father as well as the mother. At that stage a new name can be given to the child. If the parents marry at any time after 12 months of the child's birth the birth can be re-registered although the child's name cannot be changed.

Before re-registering the birth the registrar will have to be satisfied that the father agrees that he is the father. The father's consent, an affiliation order, or a further declaration by the father will be required.

To show the father of an illegitimate child

The registrar can re-register the birth at any time to name the father if:

● the mother and father jointly request it either in writing, in the form of a statutory declaration, or in person

● the mother requests it and can produce an affiliation order naming the father

If the child is over 16 years old when the request is made his or her written consent is also necessary.

Stillborn children

The law considers a baby who is born dead after the twenty-eighth week of pregnancy to be stillborn. The birth must be registered. In addition to the information required for registering a live birth the registrar will need a certificate from the doctor or midwife, who was either present at the birth or who has examined the body, stating that the child was not born alive and, if possible, the cause of death, and estimated length of pregnancy.

If neither a doctor or a midwife was present then the parent, or whoever registers the birth, will have to say that no doctor or midwife was present or has examined the body and that the child was not born alive.

Birth and death certificates will then be issued for the child.

Babies who die after birth

A baby who dies after birth will also need birth and death certificates. Again a doctor's certificate giving the cause of death is needed. The registrar must be notified within five days of the child's death. The registrar will also want to know the child's National Health number, the date and place of death, the child's usual address, the child's name and date and place of birth. The parent will then be given a death certificate and a certificate for disposal which will have to be produced to the undertaker before the baby can be buried.

Sometimes the doctor, rather than giving a certificate, will report the death to the local coroner. This is likely to happen if the death was violent or resulted from an accident, or the cause of death is not clear. In these circumstances a coroner normally arranges for a post-mortem examination to take place. If this shows that the death was from natural causes the coroner will then give a form to the parents enabling them to register the child's death.

Otherwise, an inquest will be held to establish the cause of death. Following this the coroner will send a cause of death certificate direct to the registrar so that the death can be registered.

Notification of birth

Notice of birth has to be given to the medical officer for the area or the district health authority within 36 hours of the child's birth. This is not the same as registration but is the method by which a child acquires a NHS number.

Notification can be made on prepaid forms and envelopes available from doctors or midwives. It can be made by:

● the child's father or mother

● the occupier of the house where the child was born

- anyone present at the birth
- anyone having charge of the child

Changing a child's name

No one is obliged to use the name under which they were registered. This does not, however, permit one parent to change the child's name unilaterally. There are a number of ways in which more formal arrangements can be made to change a child's name.

Within a year of birth

Parents can register a new name for the child if this is done within 12 months of the child's birth.

By statutory declaration or giving 'notice of intention'

A person, including a child, can sign a statutory declaration indicating their wish to be known by a different name or can put an advertisement in a newspaper stating that intention. These steps do not change the person's name and the name chosen by the child does not have to be used by official bodies.

By deed poll

Names can be changed by deed poll. A deed poll is a document drawn up in a particular form and signed by the person concerned.

Changing name by deed poll does not change the child's name on the Register of Births and the new name will not appear on the person's birth certificate. However, once a change of name by deed poll has been enrolled in the Central Office of the High Court in London it is accepted by most official bodies as sufficient evidence of a change of name. It will be accepted by the passport office and will be accepted by the vehicle licensing office as authority for a change of name on a person's driving licence.

It is wise to obtain the help of a solicitor in drawing up a deed poll. There is no age limit for signing a deed poll but the deed poll cannot be enrolled in the Central Register by a person under 16. Where the child is under 16 a parent or guardian of the child must enrol the deed. Where a child is between 16 and 18 the parents can still enrol the deed but the child's consent will be needed. Where parents are enrolling a deed poll on behalf of their child they must file an affidavit showing that the change of the child's name is for the child's benefit. If only one person is enrolling the deed it must be shown that the other parent consents or that there are reasons why the consent of the other parent should not be required. If the child is illegitimate the High Court, in practice, asks for the father's consent to be given.

Where a child is the subject of a parental rights resolution (see page 62) a local authority can arrange for a deed poll to change a child's name but only if the parents are dead and there is no guardian or custodian.

Restrictions on a parent changing the child's surname

Neither parent can change the child's name without the other parent's consent, if the parents are married. This still holds even if one parent has been given custody by the court.

If parents cannot agree on a change of name then the court can decide. The principle which the court will adopt is whether or not it is in the interests of the child. This can obviously be interpreted in various ways depending on the circumstances of each case.

Adoption

A child can be given new Christian names and a new surname on adoption.

Passports

A child can have a full passport at any age but cannot have a British visitors' passport until he or she is over eight years old.

Under the age of 18 a child needs the parents' consent to apply for a passport in his or her own right.

A child under 16 can travel on a parent's passport. If the parents are married the child can be included on both parents' passports. If the child is illegitimate, only the mother's can be used.

The child can only go abroad with the parent on whose passport he or she appears. Otherwise, the child will need a separate passport.

Nationality, Immigration and Emigration

British nationality and immigration law is both complicated and controversial. Over the years successive governments have reduced the rights of people from abroad to enter, remain and work in the United Kingdom. The most recent piece of legislation, the British Nationality Act 1981, which came into force on 1 January 1983, is the most restrictive of all.

It would be comforting to think that children were protected from the harshness of these laws but that is far from the case. The application of immigration and nationality laws often means that the consequences for children are bleakest of all.

Where a child is born, and to whom it is born, affects the child's nationality and status in the United Kingdom. These factors, in turn, affect the child or young person's right to enter, live in, work or study in the United Kingdom.

The law also presents particular problems for some children. They may find that their brothers and sisters have British citizenship but they do not, or that they have British citizenship but their parents may not even have the right to remain in the United Kingdom. There have been several cases recently where children who were British citizens had to return to their parents' country of origin when their parents were deemed to have no right to remain in the UK.

In addition there are special problems for children and young people born overseas who wish to come to the United Kingdom to join their families or to study. Children from the Indian subcontinent and from the West Indies face particular difficulties. British nationality and immigration laws mean that many of these children are not only separated from their families but also have to live in very deprived conditions overseas.

One of the other consequences of the present nationality laws is that some children born in the UK are now stateless—with no right to live anywhere. This is in clear breach of the

United Nations Declaration of the Rights of the Child which states clearly that every child is entitled to a nationality.

It is difficult to be optimistic about the likelihood of reform or about an improvement in the behaviour of British immigration officials. Experience does show, however, that it is worth protesting and seeking expert help. Organizations concerned with these issues are listed at the end of this book. This is a difficult area of law and expert advice should be sought. This chapter deals with the main aspects of the law as it affects children.

British citizenship

One reason why British citizenship is important is because it gives a person the right to live freely in the UK, without being subject to immigration control. There are five types of British nationality.

British citizens

British citizenship gives its holder the right to enter, remain in and leave the United Kingdom, free from any immigration control, and the right to work freely in the United Kingdom and in EEC countries.

All children born in the United Kingdom before 1 January 1983 are British citizens by birth, regardless of whether or not their parents are British citizens. The position of children born outside the United Kingdom before 1 January 1983 and of those born within the United Kingdom after 1 January 1983 is discussed below.

British Dependent Territories citizens

These are people who were born in, or reside in, or whose parents were born, registered or naturalized in a British dependent territory. This includes Bermuda, the Cayman Islands and Hong Kong. It also includes Gibraltar, but special concessions have been made for its residents who can become British citizens automatically on application. Although the Falkland Islands are a dependent territory, a special Act after the Falklands war provided that all Falklanders became British citizens.

British Dependent Territories citizens normally have the right of free entry to the dependent territory of origin. As far as the United Kingdom is concerned they have to qualify under the immigration rules before they can enter the United Kingdom or remain in it.

British overseas citizens

This group mainly consists of East African Asians or people of Chinese or Indian descent living in Malaysia. This type of British citizenship does not give the holder the right to enter and remain in the United Kingdom. Many of these people are effectively stateless.

British protected persons

British Protected Persons include those born in British Protectorates, former protectorates or trust territories, such as Uganda, Nigeria and Kenya. They do not have a right of entry into the United Kingdom.

British subjects

This group of people mainly consists of people of Indian origin who did not qualify for Indian citizenship on independence. They have no right of entry into the United Kingdom.

Effects of citizenship

The right to live and work in the United Kingdom

Only British citizenship gives an automatic right to enter, remain or leave the United Kingdom.However, there are other categories of people who have the right to live in the United Kingdom and to work.

THOSE WITH A RIGHT OF ABODE

This concept existed before the present Nationality Act came into force. Many Commonwealth citizens who came to the United Kingdom acquired right of abode. They are basically those with a parent born in the UK, and women married before 1983 to men who are British citizens. If, on 1 January 1983, a person had a right of abode in the United Kingdom, that right remains for the rest of their lives. This may be marked on a person's passport as a certificate of entitlement. This can have important consequences for their children.

Most citizens from the Commonwealth who had a right of abode became British citizens on 1 January 1983. A right of abode confers on its holder freedom from British immigration control. Permission to enter the UK is not required.

PEOPLE SETTLED IN THE UNITED KINGDOM

People who are allowed to stay permanently in the United Kingdom but are not British citizens and do not have right of abode are subject to immigration control but are allowed to remain in the United Kingdom indefinitely and to leave temporarily. This category of people includes those who came to the United Kingdom to work and had work permits and who have been allowed to remain. It also includes people who joined their parents in the UK. Settled status can be lost if a person leaves the United Kingdom for more than two years.

Some people with settled status will have their passports stamped with the words, 'Given leave to enter or remain in the United Kingdom for an indefinite period' or 'The time limit on the holder's stay is hereby revoked'.

EEC NATIONALS

Most EEC nationals have the right under the European Community legislation to freedom of movement within the EEC countries. Greek citizens will get this right in 1988; Spanish and Portuguese citizens in 1993. They can come to work and bring their families with them and can stay on after they have finished working in the UK. They are not free of immigration control but can only be refused entry or deported on grounds of public policy, public security or public health.

Children and British citizenship

It is important to remember that all children born in the United Kingdom before 1 January 1983 are automatically British citizens regardless of the nationality or legality of their parents' status in the United Kingdom. Most children born in Britain after 1 January 1983 will also be British citizens but special rules determine their status.

Children born outside the United Kingdom before 1 January 1983

A child born outside the United Kingdom before 1 January 1983 became a British citizen on that date if both the following apply:

● the child was a citizen of the United Kingdom and colonies (often referred to as CUKCs). A person falls into this category if his or her father was born, registered, naturalized or adopted before the child's birth in the UK.

● the child had the right of abode in the United Kingdom (see page 144).

Children born in the United Kingdom after 1 January 1983

A child born in the United Kingdom after 1 January 1983 will be a British citizen if: one of the child's parents or the child's mother, if the child is illegitimate, is a British citizen at the time of the child's birth, or is settled in the United Kingdom when the child is born. If the parents of an illegitimate child marry after the child is born, the child can take British citizenship from the father. This might alter the child's nationality if the father was a British citizen or settled in the United Kingdom, but the mother was not.

A newly born child who is found abandoned in the United Kingdom will be presumed to have been born to a British citizen and therefore to be a British citizen unless it can be proved otherwise. A child born in the United Kingdom after 1 January 1983 whose parent or parents are not lawfully settled, for example, if they are overseas students, or are not British citizens, will not be a British citizen.

The child will normally take the nationality of its parents although this depends on the law of the parents' country of origin. As some countries have restrictive nationality laws in relation to people born abroad this means that some children born in the United Kingdom after 1 January 1983 will be stateless. Children who are not British citizens or who are stateless may be entitled to register as British citizens (see below).

Children born outside the United Kingdom after 1 January 1983

As a general rule, British citizenship can be passed to children born abroad for one generation only. These children are said to be British citizens by descent.

A British citizen who gives birth to a child abroad transmits British citizenship to the child. If that child grows up abroad and has a child born abroad then that child will probably not be a British citizen at birth.

A special exception is made for children born abroad to a parent who is a British citizen by descent and who is working in Crown or related employment or for an EEC institution, and who was recruited in the UK. In that case as long as the child's parents are British citizens the child will be one too, regardless of how the parents acquired British citizenship.

Children born outside the UK to parents who are not British citizens will not be British citizens.

Acquiring British citizenship

There are two ways in which British citizenship can be acquired: registration and naturalization.

Registration

Children under 18 cannot acquire British citizenship by naturalization and must do so by registration. Applications for registration have to be made (normally by the child's parent or guardian, not by the child him or herself) on the citizenship registration form MN1, supplied by the Home Office. When completed, this should be sent to the Home Office or, if the child is abroad, an Embassy, Consulate or Governor. A fee is chargeable but if the family apply for registration at the same time there will only be a single fee.

The application can take a very long time to process. If it is refused, it is wise to get advice as some refusals can be challenged.

Some people have a right to registration; for others it may be up to the discretion of the Secretary of State.

CHILDREN ENTITLED TO BE REGISTERED AS BRITISH CITIZENS

A child born in the UK after 1 January 1983, who is not a British citizen at birth, will be entitled to be registered as a British citizen if one of the following applies:

- the child's parent or parents become British citizens by registration or naturalization

- one of the child's parents becomes settled in the UK (see page 144). In all cases the application for registration should be made before the child's eighteenth birthday

- the child lives lawfully in the UK for the first 10 years of his or her life and is absent for no longer than 90 days in each year. Longer absences can be ignored at the discretion of the Secretary of State

- the child is a British Dependent Territories or British Overseas Citizen, British Protected Person or British Subject by birth (see page 142), who has lived lawfully in the UK for the five years preceding the date of the application. The child must not have been absent from the country for more than 450 days in all, and not more than 90 in the year before making the application and during that year must have been settled in the UK free of immigration restrictions.

British citizenship granted in this way cannot be transmitted to the child's descendants.

CHILDREN BORN OUTSIDE THE UK TO PARENTS WHO ARE BRITISH CITIZENS BY DESCENT

If the child's parents are not resident in the UK at the time of the child's birth the child is entitled to be registered as a

British citizen within 12 months of birth if one of the following applies:

- one of the child's parents or, in the case of an illegitimate child, the mother, is a British citizen by descent

- one of the child's grandparents is, or would have been if still alive, a British citizen, either by birth, adoption, naturalization or registration

The child's parent must have lived in the UK for three years, with absences of not more than 270 days, at some point before the child was born. British citizenship granted in this way is not transmittable to the child's descendants.

If the child's family returns to the UK the child is entitled to register as a British citizen if all the following apply:

- one of the child's parents is a British citizen by descent at the time the child was born

- the child and both parents have lived in the UK for three years before the application was made and total absences from the UK in that time are not more than 270 days. If the parents have separated or divorced then the residence requirement has to be met by either, but not both, of the parents.

- both parents agree to the child being registered. In the case of legitimate children, both parents must consent even if they are separated or divorced; for illegitimate children, only the mother must consent.

This type of British citizenship *is* transmittable to the child's descendants born abroad. This means that parents in this position should think carefully about whether to register their child at birth or wait until they come back to the UK.

CHILDREN BORN OUTSIDE THE UK WHO ARE BRITISH DEPENDENT TERRITORIES CITIZENS, BRITISH OVERSEAS CITIZENS, BRITISH PROTECTED PERSONS AND BRITISH SUBJECTS

These children are entitled to be registered if they have been lawfully resident in the UK for five years and their absences abroad total not more than 450 days and have not totalled more than 90 days in the last year; and there are no immigration restrictions on their stay.

COMMONWEALTH CITIZENS AND CHILDREN
SETTLED IN THE UK BEFORE 1 JANUARY 1973

Adult Commonwealth citizens have a right to be registered. This right will continue until the end of 1987. Minors who were settled on 1 January 1973 will have a right to register for five years after their eighteenth birthday.

STATELESS CHILDREN BORN IN THE UNITED KINGDOM

Stateless children are entitled to register as British citizens, if after their birth their parent becomes a British citizen or becomes settled in the UK, or the child has lived in the UK for 10 years and has not been absent for more than 90 days in any one of those years.

In addition, there are special provisions enabling stateless children between the ages of 10 and 21 years old to register as British citizens. The following conditions must be met:

- the child must have been born in the UK or a dependent territory

- the child must have lived in the UK or a dependent territory, or partly in the United Kingdom and partly in a dependent territory for five years prior to the application. Their absences from the UK or the dependent territory must not total more than 450 days.

- during the five years in question the child must have spent more time in the UK than in the dependent territory, otherwise the child will be registered as a British Dependent Territories Citizen

- the child must be, and have always been, stateless.

STATELESS CHILDREN BORN OUTSIDE THE UNITED KINGDOM

A child in this position is entitled to be registered as a British citizen if:

- the child is and always has been stateless, and a parent, or the child's mother, if the child is illegitimate, was a British citizen when the child was born

- the child has been either in the UK or in a dependent territory for the last three years, with absences from both the United Kingdom and the dependent territory during that time not exceeding 270 days.

Discretionary registration of children

A child who is not entitled to register as a British citizen can always apply to be registered as one at the discretion of the Home Secretary. It is more likely that the Home Secretary will exercise his discretion in the child's favour if the child is resident in the UK and its future appears to be here, or if he or she has a close ancestral connection with the UK.

Entering the United Kingdom

Children and young people who are not British citizens can be subjected to rigorous and harsh immigration controls when they enter the UK, depending on whether they wish to visit, to work, to study or, most difficult of all, to settle. There are entry formalities regardless of the purpose of the visit or the country of origin.

Visas

People from some areas of the world, notably the Middle East and Africa, must obtain a visa in their country of origin before travelling to the UK. They are known as 'visa nationals' and they must have the visa before being allowed into the UK.

Entry clearance

People from countries where a visa is not required may need to obtain entry clearance before they travel, depending on the purpose of their journey. This is necessary for anyone coming to settle, but not for those coming for temporary purposes. These rules apply as much to children as they do to adults.

Visiting the UK

Children visiting the UK may have difficulties in coming to see parents who are living here and their parents will need to show that the child can be supported without the assistance of the state. Entry can be refused if the immigration authorities are not satisfied about this or think that the visit is not a genuine visit. If, for example, they feel that the young person is really coming to the UK to settle they will refuse entry.

A child coming to join parents who are working here for a limited period of time will normally be allowed to attend state schools in Britain and be treated under the National Health Service. A child coming into the country alone to study and without parents in the UK will be refused entry unless it is clear that he or she will be attending a private fee-paying school, that there is the money to pay the fees, and the child intends to leave the UK at the end of his/her studies.

Visitors are normally admitted for six months, although this period can be extended for up to a year, but no longer. Visitors are not allowed to work. Where children are joining parents who are here for a fixed period of time they will usually be allowed to stay for as long as their parents have been allowed to stay. Visitors cannot usually work unless they have work permits.

Special provisions exist for young nationals from Commonwealth countries aged between 17 and 27 who want to come to the UK to work and to have a holiday. They can be given leave to enter for up to two years as long as they have enough money for their return journey and are not reliant on public funds during their stay here. A work permit is not needed in such cases but they will not be allowed to work for the whole of their holiday. Usually they are either allowed to work part-time for the whole of their holiday or full-time for some of it.

Students

Subject to certain conditions, students can be admitted to undertake full-time studies at fee-paying schools, universities, polytechnics or other institutes of further education. They must have been accepted for a course of study which occupies the whole or a substantial part of their time, defined as being at least 15 hours per week organized day-time study. They must be able to meet the cost of studies and maintenance without having to rely on public funds, and they must intend to leave the UK at the end of their course.

Students must also obtain visas if they are visa nationals, but otherwise entry clearance is not necessary. Because it is often difficult to choose and apply for a course from abroad, the Home Office sometimes allows prospective students to be admitted for a short time to enable them to make arrangements for their studies. A young person intending to study should make this clear at the airport, rather than claiming to be a visitor. Once they have done this a student can apply to have that leave extended.

Foreign students entering the United Kingdom are likely to have to pay higher course fees than their English counterparts.

Coming to settle

The Home Office rules regarding settlement by husbands, wives and dependent children of people already settled in the UK are very strict. In many cases, these are also applied very harshly. In order to be allowed entry to the United Kingdom at all anyone wishing to settle usually has to apply for entry clearance in their country of origin.

The way in which the Home Office administers the arrangements for applications for entry has been the subject of much controversy, particularly in relation to applicants from the Indian sub-continent. In such cases there are long waits before the applicants are interviewed, and once interviewed they are treated with suspicion. It seems to be assumed by the Home Office that families from the Indian sub-continent often try and smuggle children who are not their own into the United Kingdom and consequently interviews are conducted with great attention to detail. Children will be interviewed, although those between 10 and 14 should be interviewed in the presence of an adult family relative. Discrepancies between the answers given by different family members may be enough to ensure that the application is refused. Worse still, it has now become clear that some children from the Indian sub-continent who are in fact British citizens by descent are kept waiting for entry clearance when, as British citizens, they do not need it.

Children under 18 are entitled to be admitted for settlement if one of the following applies:

- both parents are settled in the UK

- both parents are admitted for settlement at the same time as the child

- one parent is settled in the UK and the other is admittted for settlement at the same time as the child

- one parent is dead and the other parent is settled in the UK or is admitted for settlement at the same time as the child

- one parent is settled in the UK or is on the same occasion admitted for settlement and has the sole responsibility for the child's upbringing

- one parent, or a relative other than a parent, is settled or is admitted for settlement in the UK and suitable arrangements have been made for the child's care. There must also be serious considerations which make exclusion undesirable.

The child must also have a parent or sponsoring relative who is able to show that they are willing to house and maintain the child and can do so without relying on public funds. This does not apply if the parent is a Commonwealth citizen who was settled in the UK before 1973.

These rules also do not apply to EEC citizens; their families may join them freely, and only if the families are non-EEC citizens do they need entry clearance.

A single parent will have to show that he or she has had the sole responsibility for the child's upbringing, or that there are compelling family or other considerations which make exclusion undesirable. Legal custody of the child will not be enough to show that the parent has sole responsibility for the child, and the Home Office have interpreted 'compelling other reasons' very restrictively indeed.

Young people over 18 whose parents are settled in the UK cannot usually be admitted as dependants except in exceptional circumstances. These include cases where there is no other relative or where the young person is living in much poorer circumstances than generally apply in that country, or where he or she is wholly or mainly dependent on the sponsoring parent. The rules are slightly easier for unmarried daughters over the age of 18.

Emigration

If parents emigrate they have the right to take their children with them. However, this can be prevented by the courts.

A parent who objects to a child emigrating with the other parent can apply to the court. The child can apply only in exceptional circumstances. If there is a custody order (see page 26), written consent of the other parent, or the court, is required. The consent of the court is also required for a child who is a ward of court. Special provisions exist for children in local authority care (see page 73).

Adoption in the United Kingdom

Children who were adopted in the United Kingdom *before* 1 January 1983 will be British citizens if:

- they were born in the UK

- they were not UK citizens, but the person who adopted them was. If the adoption was a joint one, as most are, then it is the nationality of the adoptive father that matters. He must be a UK citizen. If he is not, then the child does not acquire British citizenship even if the mother is a British citizen. The child becomes a British citizen on the date of the adoption order.

Children who have been adopted in the UK *after* 1 January 1983 will be British citizens if:

- their natural parents (or mother if the child is illegitimate) are British citizens or settled in the UK, or

- they are legally adopted in the UK and the adopter or one of them in the case of a joint adoption is a British citizen. The child becomes a British citizen on the date the adoption order is made.

Adoption overseas

Many other countries have adoption laws and in some cases a child born and adopted abroad may later acquire British citizenship.

A child adopted overseas before 1 January 1983 will acquire British citizenship in the following cases:

- if the child was born in the UK and was validly adopted overseas and whose adoptive parent or one of them was born, adopted, registered or naturalized in the UK, or whose adopter or one of the joint adopters had been born to or legally adopted by a parent born, adopted, registered or naturalized in the UK

- where the child was a UK citizen and validly adopted outside the UK and was 'settled' for some time in the UK (see page 144) and was normally resident in the UK for the last five years or more

A child who is not a British citizen and who is adopted outside the UK after 1 January 1983 will not become a British citizen even if its adoptive parents are. The child will, however, be able to apply to be registered as a British citizen (see page 146). A child settled in the UK will be entitled to register as a British citizen after complying with the relevant residence requirements (see page 148). A child adopted abroad by parents who are British citizens and who continues to live abroad can be registered only at the discretion of the Home Secretary.

Bringing adopted children to the UK

The Home Office is concerned that the immigration rules should not be breached and tends to look suspiciously on cases where children are brought to this country to be adopted or where the adoption took place abroad but where the adopters now wish to return to the UK with their adopted child. Consequently there can be difficulties in either case.

The immigration rules state that a child adopted abroad may be brought into the UK to settle where there has been a genuine transfer of parental responsibility on the grounds that the original parents cannot care for the child and the adoption is not one arranged to enable the child to come to the UK. The adopters must also show that the child was adopted. This does not have to be a legal adoption but it must have legal force in the child's original country.

These rules have been restrictively interpreted and children have been refused entry where the authorities were not satisfied that there was sufficient evidence to show that the child's parents could not care for the child.

Likewise as Muslim law does not generally recognize adoption the Home Office have been able to say that the adoption has no legal force in the child's country of origin.

Bringing children to the UK for adoption

These cases fall into two separate categories. The first, very controversial, consists largely of childless UK couples who want to adopt a child and who cannot because of the shortage of children in the UK who are available for adoption. At the end of the Vietnam war, for example, many Vietnamese children were orphaned and some were adopted by UK nationals. Many feel that however worthy the motives of the adopters, this practice is morally wrong and that it is not in the child's long-term interests to be uprooted from the country of origin in this way.

The other type of case covers children who have come to the UK often on short stays, to live with relatives or friends who subsequently apply to adopt them. There are very great legal difficulties here.

Before an adoption order can be made in the UK the child must have been living with the adopters for at least three months, and under English adoption law at least one of the adopters must normally be resident in the UK. This will involve the child being brought to the UK first. If the adopters are British citizens they may be allowed to bring the child back to the UK but this process is difficult, expensive and likely to take some time to arrange.

The adopters must first make an application for entry to the British government's representatives in the children's country of residence. The entry clearance officer will require information about the child, e.g. date of birth, family and education. Additionally a medical certificate for the child will need to be provided. Last, but not least, the entry clearance officer will require to see evidence either that the child's parents are dead or cannot be found or that they freely consent to the adoption. The child's country of origin must also be prepared to consent or allow the adoption to go ahead. Finally the adopters must give an undertaking to notify their local social services department of their intention to apply for an adoption order as soon as the child arrives and a further undertaking that they will take financial responsibility for the child, including the cost of repatriating the child if he or she is not adopted.

Then, and only then will the child be given entry clearance to come to the UK and this is discretionary. If given, this will normally be for a period of six months which can be extended if the adoption hearing has not taken place by then.

At the adoption hearing the Home Office should be made a party to the proceedings and can oppose the making of an adoption order. When deciding whether to make the order the court has to make the child's welfare the first consideration. However, if the court feels that the true reason for making the application is the desire to give the child British citizenship then it will not make the order. In that case the child faces the prospect of being uprooted again and made to return to the country of origin.

This also applies to children who come to the UK on short stays and where the people—often relatives—who are looking after the child apply to adopt.

12 Sex

The law provides measures to protect young people from being victims of sexual abuse and is particularly concerned to protect young women. Some of the law looks rather dated in an age when girls reach puberty earlier and where sexual activity between young people is more common.

Apart from homosexuality between men, the law assumes all sexual relationships are heterosexual.

Under-age sex

Society generally views sexual activity by girls under 16 as harmful and there are several laws which can be used to protect the girl or punish the boy with whom she has had sex.

The law says that a girl under 16 cannot legally consent to sexual intercourse. This has consequences both for the girl and the man as well.

Consequences for the girl

A girl under 16 does not commit an offence by having sexual intercourse with a man and so cannot be prosecuted. However, the law can intervene in various ways.

WARDSHIP PROCEEDINGS

Wardship proceedings were often used by parents to stop their daughters continuing relationships with men where the parents thought the relationship or the man, or more commonly both, were undesirable. The wardship court has very great powers to regulate the life of a young woman in these circumstances although it is slower to act today than before. This type of case has become less common recently but the court has not lost its power to intervene if asked to do so. If a girl's parents make her a ward of court in these circumstances she should ask the court to appoint the Official Solicitor to act for her so that her views can be put to the court (see page 12).

CARE PROCEEDINGS

In extreme cases the local authority could bring proceedings to take the girl into care (see Chapter 5) on the grounds that she was in moral danger. If the local authority refuse to take care proceedings the girl's parents can apply to the juvenile court to force them to do so. In practice local authorities only seem to take care proceedings where the sexual relationship is incestuous or the girl has run away from home. If the girl was having a lesbian relationship the local authority may also bring care proceedings, and would be likely to do so if the girl's parents asked them to. The girl will normally have her own solicitor who should put her views to the court (see page 60).

Consequences for the man

Although the girl has not committed an offence, the man can be prosecuted in a variety of ways. A boy under 14 is presumed by the law to be incapable of having sexual intercourse but could still be prosecuted for indecent assault.

UNLAWFUL SEXUAL INTERCOURSE

Any boy or man who is over 14 and has sex with a girl under 13 will be guilty of unlawful sexual intercourse. If the girl was between 13 and 16, the man will not be guilty if he was under 24 when intercourse took place *and* he believed the girl was over 16. He cannot use this defence if he has been convicted of the same offence before.

INDECENT ASSAULT

Indecent assault is an offence whatever the age of those concerned. Indecent assault on a girl under 16, however, is considered more serious and the courts have power to inflict higher penalties if the man is convicted.

TAKING A GIRL AWAY FROM HER PARENTS

It is an offence to take a girl away from her parents without their consent if she is under 16 (and in some circumstances if the girl is between 16 and 18). This is a crime even if there is no question of sexual intercourse taking place but in practice usually involves a boyfriend and girlfriend running away together.

USING PREMISES FOR SEXUAL INTERCOURSE

Anyone who lets a girl under 16 use their property for sexual intercourse commits an offence. This applies to anyone even if they do not have intercourse with the girl themselves. If a man and girl run away and stay with friends, the friends will have committed an offence.

Contraception and abortion where the girl is under 16

In certain circumstances girls under 16 can be prescribed contraception by a doctor without the consent or knowledge of their parents (see page 19).

Teenage sex

Consequences for the woman

Sex where the young woman is between 16 and 18 also has legal implications. Although a woman can legally give her consent to intercourse and can leave home without her parents' consent this does not stop the local authority bringing care proceedings on the grounds that she is in moral danger (see above). If a care order is made when a girl is over 16 it can last until she is 19.

The fact that a girl is over 16 does not prevent her parents taking wardship proceedings. She will cease to be a ward of court on her eighteenth birthday and any orders the court has made will end.

Consequences for the man

A man who takes an unmarried girl who is under 18 away from her parents without their consent is guilty of an offence *if* he takes her in order to have sexual intercourse. The man can only avoid being convicted if he can show he thought the young woman was over 18.

Young men and sex

The age of consent does not apply to men, who can lawfully consent to sexual intercourse at any age. However, young men under 14 are presumed to be incapable of sexual intercourse. A young man who has intercourse with a girl under 16 will be committing an offence (see page 159).

Homosexual relationships

Lesbian relationships are not illegal. However, if a woman over 16 entered into a relationship with a girl under 16, or if the girl did not consent, the woman could be prosecuted for indecent assault.

In the case of men, the law states that all homosexual relationships are illegal unless:

● the participants are 21 or over

● the sexual act is in private and the participants consent

Where prosecutions are brought, these are usually for gross indecency or buggery. Buggery means anal intercourse; gross indecency covers any homosexual act other than buggery. If young men are prosecuted for homosexual relationships, they can be taken into care.

Boys under 14 cannot be prosecuted since they are presumed by the law to be incapable of intercourse. Those under 16 are presumed to be incapable of consenting to homosexual relationships and so cannot be prosecuted either, although if their partner were older, he could be prosecuted. A young man could still be prosecuted for indecent assault.

Rape

Rape is committed when a man has sexual intercourse with a woman who is not his wife, when she does not consent and he knows that she doesn't, or doesn't care whether or not she does. The offence can be committed even though full sexual intercourse has not taken place—penetration, however slight, will do. Nor is it necessary for ejaculation to have taken place. Rape is regarded by the law as a very serious offence and is punishable with life imprisonment.

A woman cannot commit rape. She can, however, be prosecuted for indecent assault or for aiding and abetting a man to commit rape. A young man cannot commit rape if he is under 14 years old.

Incest

Incest is thought to be much more common than the number of prosecutions would suggest. It is a horrifying crime which is easily concealed and which can be very difficult to prove.
Incest can have devastating consequences for families. Where the father commits incest, it is often the mother that suffers most but many children never recover emotionally from the experience.

Incestuous relationships between father and daughter are the most common although the definition of incest is much wider than that. A man commits incest if he has sexual intercourse with his daughter, granddaughter, sister, half-sister or mother. The man is guilty of the offence even if the woman consents. A woman commits incest if she is over 16 and allows a man to have sexual intercourse with her and he is her father, grandfather, brother, half-brother or son.

The maximum penalty is seven years' imprisonment. However, if a man commits the offence with a girl under 13 years it is life imprisonment. It is also an offence for a man or woman to attempt to commit incest or to encourage a girl to have sexual intercourse where that would be incest. If someone is convicted of incest the criminal court can take that person's parental rights away from them.

In families where incest has been committed the local authority will often take care or wardship proceedings in respect of the child. If successful, the local authority or the court may only let the child back home if the mother complies with very strict conditions, such as never letting the child see her father again.

Children do not have to endure incestuous relationships. They should seek outside assistance if there is no one inside the family who can help. Social workers and teachers treat complaints of incest seriously and the law gives local authorities wide powers to protect children in these circumstances (see Chapter 5).

Contraception

Some forms of contraception are available without prescription, including condoms and spermicides. These, however, tend to be among the least effective methods. Other contraceptives, such as the pill, the cap and the coil, are only available on prescription.

The whole area has recently been the subject of much controversy because of the case brought by Mrs Gillick. She objected to girls being given contraceptive advice and treatment without their parents' knowledge and consent. She lost the case.

As a result of the decision in this case, girls under 16 can now obtain contraceptive advice and treatment without their parents' knowledge or consent in certain circumstances (see page 19).

Young women over the age of 16 can obtain contraceptive advice and treatment without parental consent.

Children, Young People and the Police

Children and young people can come into contact with the police in a number of ways. This chapter explains what happens when children are stopped, searched, arrested or detained by the police. In such circumstances, the police have certain duties and children certain rights.

The rights of children in these types of cases are much the same as those of adults. Although the powers of the police have recently been extended most of the safeguards for children are not part of the new laws but are contained in codes of practice issued by the government. The police should abide by these codes but it is uncertain how they can be enforced legally.

The power to stop and search

Police powers to search are limited unless someone has been arrested, or consents to being searched. The police can stop and search anyone or any vehicle for stolen goods or prohibited articles. They may detain the person in order to carry out the search. The police must have reasonable grounds for suspecting that the person has what they are looking for.

Prohibited articles

These include offensive weapons. An offensive weapon is anything designed to cause injury to a person, such as a gun, or anything which is intended to be used to cause injury, whether it was originally made for that purpose or not. A hammer, a kitchen knife, or even an umbrella could be an offensive weapon.

Other prohibited articles are those made, adapted, or intended to be used to commit burglary, theft, taking a vehicle without permission, or obtaining property by deception. Items covered by this part of the law could include forged cheque cards, car keys, jemmys and false pockets in coats or shopping bags.

Reasonable grounds

The police must have reasonable grounds for believing that a person has stolen or prohibited goods in their possession before they can stop and search. They cannot stop people because of their colour or the way they dress. Nor can they act on a hunch.

Where people can be stopped and searched

This can be done in any public place to which the public has access, including parks, sports grounds and cinemas. Not included are private yards or gardens unless the police have reasonable grounds for believing the person who is to be searched does not live there or is there without the owner's or resident's permission. This means they could search someone who was hiding in a yard.

Police duties on searching

The law also says that officers who stop and intend to search must identify themselves, show warrant cards if not in uniform, and give their names and the police station to which they are attached. They must also state the reason for the search and what they are looking for.

Police officers must make a written record of the search. They should also tell the person who is stopped that they are entitled to a copy of this record if they ask for it within a year.

Arrest

Arresting someone entitles the police to detain them against their will. The person will usually then be taken to a police station and detained or charged. If charged, they will then be brought before the court (see Chapter 14).

The law on arrest is complicated. Depending on the circumstances, the police can arrest someone with or without a warrant. Alternatively, people can be summonsed and brought before the court without being arrested at all. If a warrant is needed to arrest somebody the police must first apply to a magistrate for one.

Arrest without a warrant

The police can arrest someone without a warrant in any of the following circumstances:

● if they suspect an arrestable offence has been, is being, or is about to be committed. An arrestable offence is one for which an adult could be sentenced to at least five years' imprisonment. This includes theft, criminal damage, robbery or burglary.

● where other offences designated as arrestable offences have been, are being or are about to be committed. These are smuggling and unlawful importation of goods, possession of prohibited drugs, indecent assault on a woman, causing or arranging prostitution, taking and driving away a vehicle, going equipped for theft, corruption, or some offences under the Official Secrets Act.

● where parliament has given the police the power to arrest without a warrant. There are many provisions here including offences under the Public Order Acts and driving while unfit or disqualified to do so.

● if the police officer has reasonable grounds for suspecting a person of attempting or committing an offence and cannot establish the person's name or address. This holds if the officer believes that the name given is false, or that the person will not stay at the address given for long enough to enable a summons to be served. This condition also covers cases where the officer believes that the arrest is necessary to prevent the person causing injury or harm to themselves or others, damage to property, or an offence against public decency, or an unlawful obstruction of the highway, or to protect a child or other vulnerable person from the suspect.

Arrests for fingerprinting

Certain new provisions enable the police to arrest a person if they have already been convicted of certain offences and have not had their fingerprints taken or complied with a request to go to a police station to have them taken. This is likely to be used only in very rare circumstances.

A request for fingerprints must be made within one month of the date of conviction. The person has at least seven days in which to go to the police station to give the fingerprints.

What the police must do on arrest

The police must inform a person that they are under arrest, either when they are arrested, or as soon as is possible afterwards. The police must also say why they have made the arrest. The law says that an arrested person should be taken to the police station as soon as possible. But the police have the power to take the person somewhere else to help them with their investigation. The rules about how long people can be detained in police stations do not start to operate until the person arrives at the police station (see page 168).

Searching arrested people

In addition to the stop and search powers, the police have the power to search people when they are arrested. They can do so if they have reasonable grounds for believing that the arrested person may be a danger to himself or others, or may have concealed on their person anything which could be used to escape, or which might be evidence of an offence.

In any search that takes place in public no clothing, apart from an overcoat, jacket or gloves can be removed. An officer can take items found on a person who has been arrested but only if he reasonably believes that it falls into the categories set out above.

The police also have powers to search premises where the arrested person was when arrested or immediately before the arrest, if they have reasonable grounds for believing there is evidence on the premises relating to the offence.

After the arrest

Once a person is brought to the police station they must either be charged if there is sufficient evidence, or released, either unconditionally or on bail. If there is not sufficient evidence to charge the person, the police may wish to make further enquiries. They will then have to decide whether to release the person on bail or detain them while enquiries are made.

If enquiries are likely to take a long time, for example, where someone is arrested in possession of a substance the police suspect to be prohibited drugs and which needs to be analyzed, the police will usually release the person on bail and ask them to come back to the police station on another day, when the analysis has been completed.

Detention

Detention after being charged

A person who is charged does not have to be released if the custody officer:

- does not know their name and address or believes either of these to be false

- has reasonable cause to believe that the detention is necessary to protect that person or someone else or someone else's property

- has reasonable grounds to believe that the person will fail to appear in court, or if released would interfere with the investigation of a criminal offence

If the young person is under 17 they can also be detained if the police believe it is in the young person's own interests.

If a young person is charged but not released, the police must make arrangements for the young person to be transferred to the care of the local authority, unless this is 'impracticable'. The police should not use the young person's behaviour or the nature of the offence as a reason for saying it is impracticable.

The police are not generally allowed to question someone about an offence after they have been charged with it.

Detention without being charged

People who are not charged should be released unless the custody officer believes their detention is necessary, either to secure or preserve evidence relating to the offence for which the person was arrested, or to obtain such evidence by questioning.

The length of time for which a suspect can be detained depends on whether the offence is a serious arrestable offence or not. Serious arrestable offences include murder, manslaughter, rape and indecent assault, or any arrestable offence if it has led or is likely to lead to any of the following consequences:

● serious harm to the security of the state or public order

● serious interference with the administration of justice or the investigation of an offence

● the death of, or serious injury to, a person

● substantial financial gain to any person

● or serious financial loss.

Lengths of periods of detention

Anyone arrested for any offence can be detained for up to 24 hours before being charged. During that period the custody officer will regularly review the necessity for detention. The detained person or their representatives should normally be allowed to put their views. At the end of that time the person must be released, or charged, unless they are suspected of committing a serious arrestable offence.

In the case of a serious arrestable offence the period of detention can be extended to 36 hours on the authorization of a senior police officer. There must be reasonable grounds for believing that detention is necessary to secure or preserve evidence, or to obtain evidence. The investigation must be conducted speedily.

Further detention without charge requires the approval of the magistrates' court. Magistrates' courts can extend detention for a further 36 hours on the first application. A second application can also be made. The period of detention can be up to 96 hours in total. A person is entitled to be legally represented on such applications.

At the police station

Questioning

The law itself says nothing about how young people should be questioned. The code of practice which the government has issued does, however, state that young people should not be interviewed or asked to make a signed or written statement unless one of the following is present:

● a parent or guardian, or representative from the care authority if the young person is in care

● a social worker

● another responsible adult who is not a police officer

This condition does not apply where the police consider that the delay would involve an immediate risk of harm to others or a serious loss of, or damage to, property.

Confessions obtained by the police at the station can be excluded in subsequent court proceedings if the court thinks they are unreliable or were obtained as a result of harassment.

Searches

Custody officers must make a written record of all property that a detained person has in their possession. They can also search them. This can be a strip search, that is, a search which involves the removal of more than outer clothing.

Strip searches can only be carried out by an officer of the same sex as the person detained. No one else, other than a doctor, should be present. The reason for such a search and its result must be recorded.

The police can hold any property that a person has in their possession, but can only keep clothes and personal effects if they have reasonable grounds for believing that these may be used to cause physical injury, to damage property, to interfere with evidence, or to assist in an escape.

Intimate searches

Intimate searches involve the examination of a body orifice. They can only be carried out if a senior officer has reasonable grounds for believing that the arrested person has concealed any item which could cause themselves injury, or has concealed a Class A drug. This includes heroin and cocaine. The police must have reasonable grounds for believing that the person possesses it with intent to supply someone else with it or to export it, and that such a search is necessary to find the item.

An intimate search for drugs must be carried out by a doctor or a nurse, at a hospital, doctor's surgery, or other medical premises. In exceptional circumstances, an intimate search for a dangerous item can be carried out at the police station by a police officer.

If a young person under 17 is to be searched in this way, an adult of the same sex must be present, unless the young person does not wish the adult to be there and the adult agrees. This can be a parent, guardian, representative of the care authority if the young person is in care, social worker or another responsible adult who is not a police officer. The police can use reasonable force in carrying out any search.

Access to legal advice

Anyone who is detained has a right to communicate and consult privately with a solicitor at any time. The police can delay this for up to 36 hours if someone is detained for a serious arrestable offence and they think that would interfere with evidence, lead to harm to others, alert other people suspected of a serious arrestable offence or hinder the recovery of property obtained as a result of such an offence.

Informing parents

The police must take all practicable steps to find out who is responsible for the welfare of an arrested young person. This also applies if the young person suffers from mental handicap or illness. They must then inform that person of the arrest, give the reasons why, and the address of the place where they are detained, as soon as practicable. If the young person is on a supervision order, the supervisor should also be informed and given that information. The police cannot delay in doing this as they can for access to legal advice.

In addition, anybody in police custody has the right to have a friend or relative informed of the arrest or detention. This can be postponed for up to 36 hours in the same way as can access to legal advice.

Types of identification

The police can take photographs, fingerprints and body samples from young people in certain cases but only with the appropriate consent. If a child is aged between 10 and 13 the consent of the parent or guardian is required. In the case of 14- to 16-year-olds, the consent of the arrested person and his or her parent or guardian is required.

Fingerprints

Before fingerprinting young people the police should normally obtain the written appropriate consent of the person concerned. Children under 10 years old cannot be fingerprinted. The police can dispense with the appropriate consent if they believe that the young person is involved in a criminal offence and fingerprints will prove or disprove this. They can also dispense with consent if the young person has been charged with or convicted of certain offences called recordable offences and has not had their fingerprints taken in the course of the investigations. Reasonable force may be used to take fingerprints.

If fingerprints are taken, and the person concerned is cleared, not prosecuted or cautioned, or not suspected of the offence relating to which they were taken then the fingerprints must be destroyed. The person concerned can ask to witness their destruction.

Photographs

Normally the police need to get written consent before taking photographs of young persons. They may be taken without consent if a young person is arrested at the same time as others and a photograph is necessary to establish who was arrested at what time and what place. Consent can also be dispensed with if the person is charged with, or reported for, certain offences and has not yet been released or brought before a court, or if they are convicted of such an offence and their photograph is not already on record.

Force may not be used to take photographs. The right to have photographs destroyed is the same as that for fingerprints.

Body samples

In certain circumstances body samples can be taken. These include samples of blood, urine, saliva, semen, or genital or rectal swabs, known as 'intimate body samples'. Samples can also be taken of nails and hair.

In the case of young people, samples can only usually be taken with appropriate written consent. Non-intimate body samples can be taken without consent if authorized by a police superintendent who suspects the person of a serious arrestable offence and believes the sample will tend to prove or disprove their involvement.

Intimate body samples cannot be taken without consent. Apart from samples of saliva or urine, these must be taken by a doctor.

Identification procedures

These should take place in the presence of an adult and with the appropriate adult's consent. There are particular rules for carrying out identification parades designed to make them fair. It is wise to obtain help from a solicitor if possible before agreeing to a parade.

Cautioning

As an alternative to charging a young person with an offence the police can caution them. A caution consists of a 'firm talking to' by a senior police officer. This usually takes place at the police station and should be in the presence of the young person's parent or guardian.

Whether or not the police give a caution is, at the end of the day, up to them. Normally, however, four conditions must be met before the police will administer a caution. These are:

- the police have enough evidence to prosecute the young person

- the young person admits the offence

- the parents or guardian agree to the caution being administered

- the police take the victim's wishes into account

Even if all these conditions are met the police can still prosecute. Practice varies from police authority to authority. The decision is usually referred to the Juvenile Bureau who will make further enquiries about the young person's background. They may visit the young person's parents, or make enquiries with the social services or education department before recommending a caution or charge.

Although a caution avoids prosecution and possible conviction, cautions can be read out later if a young person is subsequently convicted of another offence (see page 180). One criticism of cautioning is that young people may be persuaded to admit something they haven't done in order to avoid being taken to court. Legal advice should be sought before agreeing to a caution.

In some areas the matter will now be dealt with by a multi-agency panel composed of representatives from the police, social services, the local education authority, the probation service, etc, who discuss whether the young person should be cautioned or prosecuted.

Criminal Offences

Society has ambivalent attitudes towards children who commit crimes. Much of the law in this area is the subject of controversy. Up to the nineteenth century children could be convicted of criminal offences from the age of seven on and were often punished as severely as adults. Today the age of responsibility is 10. In 1969 a law was passed raising the age to 14, but that law has never been brought into force. It does not look as though it will be in the forseeable future.

Children and young people do break the law in large numbers. They make up a significant proportion of the total numbers of those convicted of criminal offences. However, society has not been able to come to a clear decision as to how to deal with young offenders. Sentences range from those aimed at helping or 'treating' children to real punishment. Some of the sentences available to courts for young people are harsher than adult sentences. For example, children can be 'sentenced' to a care order which can in practice mean a lengthy period in an institution.

The age of criminal responsibility

For a court to convict anyone of a criminal offence it is usually necessary for the prosecution to show firstly that the offence itself has been committed. For example, the prosecution must show that the person charged did physically take the goods in question. Secondly, the prosecution must show that the person intended to do it and knew that it was wrong. Because it is accepted that young children do not understand right and wrong in the same way as adults, no child under 10 can be convicted of a criminal offence.

Between the ages of 10 and 14 a child can be convicted of a criminal offence but the law still presumes that the child does not know the difference between right and wrong. Consequently, if a child between 10 and 14 is prosecuted, he or she should not be convicted unless the prosecution can show that the child was in fact aware that what was done was wrong. This presumption gradually diminishes the nearer a child gets to 14, until when a child is 14, it disappears altogether.

Differences between adults and children

There are other differences between the way in which children and young people and adults are dealt with in relation to criminal offences. Children are usually tried in different courts, in different procedures. They do not have the right to choose to be tried by a judge and jury and, if convicted, they are dealt with in different ways.

The criminal law calls those between the age of 10 and 14 children, those between 14 and 17 young people. They are often collectively called 'juveniles'. Over 17 they are treated as adults by the criminal law. In this section the term 'juveniles' will be used if both children and young people are concerned.

Which court?

A juvenile charged with a criminal offence is normally dealt with in the juvenile court. There are certain exceptions.

If he or she is charged jointly with an adult, both will be tried at the magistrates' court. If the court considers it necessary in the interests of justice to send both of them to trial at the crown court, or the adult chooses to be tried at the crown court then the case will be heard at the crown court. If a juvenile is tried in the magistrates' court or the crown court then normally he or she will be sent back to the juvenile court for sentencing if found guilty.

A magistrates' court must send any juvenile found guilty back to the juvenile court unless it feels that the case can properly be dealt with by means of an absolute or conditional discharge, by a fine or by binding over the juvenile's parent or guardian (see page 181). This applies to a young person who has become an adult during the course of the case.

If a juvenile is charged with an adult and the adult pleads guilty but the juvenile does not, the magistrates' court can sometimes send the case back to the juvenile court for trial.

If the juvenile is charged with homicide, the case must be tried by a judge and jury at the crown court.

If a young person between 14 and 17 is charged with an offence for which an adult could be sent to prison for 14 years or more, including robbery or rape, for example, the court can send the young person for trial at the crown court if it feels that they might deserve or need a longer sentence of detention than is available in a juvenile court. There is evidence that some juvenile courts are increasingly sending young people who are charged with robbery and burglary to the crown court for trial.

Coming before the court

Many juveniles charged with criminal offences will be 'summonsed' to go to the juvenile court. A summons is a notice which orders the person to turn up at court on a particular day.

If the child or young person does not attend court a warrant can be issued for their arrest. It is important to let the court know if there is some reason why attendance is impossible. The warrant will stipulate whether bail should be given by the police once the person has been arrested.

In some circumstances a child or young person may be arrested by the police, released on bail and told when to go to court.

Adjournments

Often the court cannot hear the case on the day on which the young person has been asked to attend. In that case they will adjourn it to another day. This is often called a remand. Usually magistrates would grant a young person bail which means that they are released from the court and told to come back on the next date that has been set. Failure to attend court when on bail is a separate offence which carries its own penalties.

Bail

The juvenile court can refuse to grant a juvenile bail, but only if satisfied that one of the following applies:

● that the juvenile would not come back to court for the case

● that he or she would commit offences while on bail

● that he or she would interfere with witnesses or obstruct the course of justice

● that it is in the juvenile's interests to be kept in custody

If bail is refused, an application for bail can be made to the crown court. Legal advice should be sought.

Remand in care

Where a juvenile is not released on bail he or she must be committed to the care of the local authority unless the court makes an unruliness certificate.

Unruliness certificates

In certain circumstances, a boy, aged between 14 and 17 years who is not given bail can be made the subject of an 'unruliness certificate'. This means that he will not be remanded in the care of the local authority but will be detained at a remand centre or sometimes a prison for up to 28 days.

The court can only make an unruliness certificate if it feels that the boy cannot be committed to the care of the local authority safely and one of the following conditions applies:

● the young person is charged with an offence for which an adult could be sent to prison for more than 14 years

● the young person has been charged with an offence of violence or has been found guilty of an offence of violence on a previous occasion

● the young person has persistently run away from a community home, or seriously disrupted the running of the community home

● and in any of the above cases the court is satisfied on the basis of a report from the local authority that there is no

community home to which the young person could be sent
without the risk of disrupting it.

When a young person first comes before the court, the court can
make an unruliness certificate even though there is no report from
the local authority, as long as there has not been enough time to
prepare one. The government proposes to restrict the use of
unruliness certificates to serious crimes only such as rape and
murder.

Procedure at the juvenile court

One or both parents should attend court with their child. If not,
the case may be put off until another day.

The charge

The court should begin by explaining to the juvenile what it is
that he or she is accused of doing. This explanation should be
given in simple language, capable of being understood by a child.

After the charge has been explained the juvenile should be asked
whether or not he or she admits the charge. If the charge is
admitted, the court will go on to consider what sentence to give
(see page 180). If not then the court must decide whether he or
she is guilty. The case will then be conducted in much the same
way as a criminal trial in the magistrates' court. It is advisable for
children and young people to get legal advice, especially if they
are denying the charge. If there has not been time to get legal
advice, then the court can be asked to adjourn the case.

The evidence

The case will begin with the prosecution making a speech and
calling witnesses to give evidence in support of its case. Each
witness gives evidence orally and can then be cross-examined by
the child's lawyer. If the juvenile has no lawyer, then parents can
help the child conduct the case.

At the end of the prosecution's evidence the defence may
sometimes ask the court to dismiss the case because the prosecution
have not proved it. More often the child's lawyer will go on to

call witnesses in support of his or her case. The child may also be called but this is not obligatory. The defence does not have to call any evidence at all if it does not wish to. At the end of all the evidence the defence lawyer will make a speech and the magistrates will then decide whether or not they find the juvenile guilty.

If the juvenile is found guilty or has admitted the offence

Before the court can decide what to do it has to take into account information about the juvenile's background. The procedure at this stage is different from that in adult courts. The local authority has a duty to make investigations and provide the court with information about a juvenile's home surroundings, school record, health and character. If this information is not available the court can adjourn the case for reports to be prepared.

Usually the court will want reports from the local authority. In some cases the probation service and the juvenile's school may also be called upon. Such reports do not have to be shown to the juvenile or his parents, but, if they are not, the child and the parents must be told about those parts of the report which the court considers to be relevant to the case. Increasingly, reports are shown.

Before the court decides how to deal with the case the juvenile and his parents should be given an opportunity of making a statement to the court. Some courts are much better than others at discussing the matters with the juvenile and his or her parents. Some courts are so intimidating that few children or their parents feel able to speak.

Before dealing with the case the court will want to know if the juvenile has any previous convictions or cautions (see page 174) and will take these into account when deciding what sentence to impose.

Orders the court can make

The juvenile court has very different powers from adult courts when it comes to deciding what orders, or sentences, to make.

Absolute or conditional discharge

These are alternatives to punishing a juvenile. If an absolute discharge is ordered, no punishment can be imposed later for the offence.

A conditional discharge can last for up to three years. If a further offence is committed within that period, the juvenile can be brought back to court and punished for the original offence as well as the subsequent one.

Absolute and conditional discharges do not count as convictions, except where a further offence is committed while a conditional discharge is still in operation.

Binding over

A parent of a young person aged over 14 who is convicted of an offence can be bound over by the court. This means that they promise the court to exert proper control over the child under threat of losing a specified sum of money. If they do not, then they can be brought back to court and fined a sum of money, up to £1,000. The bind-over period cannot be longer than three years and will, in any event, run out when the young person reaches the age of 18.

A child or young person can also be bound over to be of good behaviour. This is very rarely done.

Deferring sentence

The juvenile court can postpone passing sentence for a period of up to six months. It will usually do this to give the child or young person concerned an opportunity to show that they have kept out of trouble. The court can then impose whatever order it sees fit at the end of that time. Conditions are normally placed on the deferment. These always include a condition not to commit any further offence, but may also involve a promise to attend school regularly or to save towards paying compensation for the offence. If the conditions are kept, particularly the offence condition, the juvenile can expect to be dealt with leniently when sentence is passed. Because it is a sort of bargain between the juvenile and the court, the juvenile concerned must consent to sentence being deferred.

Fines

The juvenile court can impose a fine of up to £400 for a young person over 14 or £100 in the case of a child under 14. The court must order that the fine be paid by the child's parent or guardian, unless they cannot be found or it would be unreasonable to do so.

Supervision orders

Supervision orders can be made in care and criminal proceedings. Some conditions, however, can only be imposed in criminal cases.

A supervision order places a child or young person under the supervision of either the local authority's social services department or a probation officer. It can be made whether or not the child or young person consents.

A supervising officer's duties are to advise, assist and befriend a child or young person. They will normally require to see the child or young person at regular intervals. A probation officer can only be appointed as a supervisor if the child is aged at least 13, the local authority requests it, and the probation officer is already involved in the household.

A supervision order lasts for up to three years. When it is made in criminal proceedings it can last beyond the child's eighteenth birthday.

The juvenile has to inform the supervisor at once of any change of address or employment. He or she also must keep in touch with the supervisor in accordance with instructions and allow the supervisor to visit.

MEDICAL TREATMENT

A supervision order can also specify that the child or young person receives treatment for a mental illness. The court can only make this a requirement if a medical practitioner has certified that the condition of the child or young person warrants such treatment. The doctor must also state that the juvenile would be susceptible to treatment but that detention in hospital is not necessary.

A young person who is 14 years or over has to consent before such a condition is made. The court must specify the length of time for treatment. This cannot extend beyond the person's eighteenth birthday.

INTERMEDIATE TREATMENT

Intermediate treatment consists of certain specific requirements or conditions added to a supervision order. The purpose of intermediate treatment is to help children without removing them from home.

The court may leave the specifics of treatment up to the supervising officer. This is sometimes known as 'delegated intermediate treatment'. The court or supervisor specify where the child should live and that the child should participate in a timetable of activities to be chosen by the supervisor. It is then up to the supervisor to decide what directions, if any, to give. The court, however, cannot make an order unless it is satisfied that a scheme of intermediate treatment is already in force in the area where the child or young person lives. The maximum period such directions can last is 90 days. The court can order shorter times.

OTHER CONDITIONS

The court can make additional requirements. These are:

● that the juvenile does anything that the supervisor has power or would have power to direct him to do

● that the juvenile remains for a specified period between 6 pm and 6 am at a specified place or places. This is known as a 'night restriction order'. One of the places specified must be the place where the juvenile lives. The order cannot require the juvenile to remain at a place for longer than 10 hours on any one night, and cannot be imposed for more than three months from the date of the order or last for more than 30 days.

The juvenile can leave the place during the hours on which the night restriction applies if he is accompanied by his parent or guardian, his supervisor or by someone else specified in the supervision order.

The juvenile can also be told not to participate in specified activities during the whole, part of, or on particular days while the order is in force.

Before imposing such conditions the court must be satisfied that the child will comply with the conditions and that they are necessary in order to secure the child's good behaviour or to prevent a repetition of the offence. The court can only impose these conditions if the young person agrees, or if the child is under 14, if the parents agree. These conditions can only be imposed where the child has been convicted of an offence.

BREACH OF SUPERVISION

Failure to comply with conditions made in a supervision order in criminal proceedings can result in the juvenile being brought back before the court and punished by:

● a fine

● an attendance centre order

● the imposition of another sentence if the young person has reached the age of 18.

VARYING AND DISCHARGING SUPERVISION ORDERS

The supervisor or the juvenile can apply to the court to have the supervision order discharged or to have new conditions laid down. The court can also make a care order in its place.

Care orders

The court can make a care order if the young person is over 14 and has been found guilty of a crime for which an adult could be sent to prison. This covers most offences. Where a child is aged between 10 and 14 the court can only make a care order if the child has been found guilty of homicide (but see page 57).

Before making a care order the court has to be satisfied that it is the appropriate action to take and that unless the order is made the child or young person would be unlikely to receive proper care and control. The court should not make a care order unless the juvenile is legally represented or has refused or failed to apply for legal aid.

Care orders made in criminal proceedings last until the young person is 18, unless he or she is over 16 when the order is made, when it lasts until the child is 19. An application can be made to discharge the care order by the child, or on the child's behalf by a parent, guardian, or the local authority. A care order places the juvenile in the care of the local authority who decides where the juvenile should live. This may be in a children's home, community home or even at home. If a child in care commits another offence the court can stop the local authority sending the juvenile home or to relatives, or order that if he or she does go to live with a parent or relative, who that should be. Such an order can only last for a specified time and not for longer than 6 months.

Attendance centre order

Attendance centres are places where young people under the age of 21 can be ordered to go to take part in specified activities. The court can make an attendance centre order where a child or young person is found guilty of an offence for which an adult could be sent to prison.

The court must specify the number of hours to be served at the attendance centre. This cannot be less than 12 hours a day, unless the child is under 14 and 12 hours would be considered too much. It should not be more than 12 hours, unless that is thought to be inadequate. In that case the court can order up to 24 hours, or up to 36 hours if the person is over 17.

The court will specify the first time when the child or young person must attend the centre but, after that, the times will be laid down by the person in charge of the centre. Attendance centres are usually open at weekends, particularly Saturday afternoons. Physical training exercises are common activities. One of the aims of attendance centres is to keep young people out of trouble and hours are often organized to coincide with football matches. This order is commonly made when someone has been convicted of offences connected with football hooliganism.

Failure to attend an attendance centre or to comply with the attendance centre's rules can be dealt with by the court. Another sentence can be imposed instead.

Detention centres

Detention centres are often described as providing a 'short, sharp shock' for juvenile offenders. They are custodial and vary in the type of regime imposed, although all have a highly disciplined, and many would say, very harsh system involving hard physical work, parades, inspections and a strict system of punishment. Only boys can be sent to detention centres. Evidence shows that, despite the harshness of the regime, detention centres are no more effective than anything else in preventing young people re-offending.

Boys can be sent to a detention centre if they are over 14 and under 21 and have been convicted of an offence for which an adult could be sent to prison. The court must think that this is the only appropriate method of dealing with the child and that no more than four months in custody is required.

The court must also be satisfied that the child's mental and physical health do not make him unfit for such a sentence. For this reason, the court will ask that the child be medically examined before sentencing him to a detention centre.

The court sets the limit to be served in the detention centre. It cannot be more than four months, or less than 21 days, unless the detention centre order is made because the child has broken the terms of a supervision order. In that case, it can be less. After release, the young person should be supervised by a probation officer for between three and 12 months.

Youth custody

Until recently young people could not be sentenced to terms of imprisonment although they could be sent to detention centres or borstals. Since 1982, young people can be sentenced to youth custody which should be served in special youth custody centres. However, because the number of places in such centres is limited and many young people are sentenced to youth custody, some young people have to serve their sentences in adult prisons or in adult remand centres. Unlike adult prison sentences, youth custody cannot be suspended.

A youth custody sentence can only be passed if the offender is between 15 and 20 inclusive (boys) or 17 and 20 inclusive (girls). The offence must be one for which an adult could be sentenced to prison and the court must feel that the only appropriate way of dealing with the person is a custodial sentence of more than four months. In the case of a boy, the sentence can be less than four months if his medical or physical condition makes a detention centre unsuitable or if he has already served a period of imprisonment, youth custody or detention. Girls can also be sentenced to less than four months.

Normally youth custody orders must be for more than four months and less than 12 months, although the magistrates or juvenile court can only impose a maximum of six months for any one offence. In order to receive a sentence of more than six months, the young person will need to have been convicted of more than one offence.

If the court thinks that a longer custodial sentence is necessary, it can send the young person to the crown court. This can only be done if the young person is over 15.

Detention at Her Majesty's Pleasure (Imprisonment)

This custodial sentence can only be imposed where a child is convicted of murder and was under 18 at the time the offence was committed. In such a case the court must sentence the child to be detained at Her Majesty's Pleasure.

Longer custodial sentences

Longer custodial sentences can be imposed where a child or young person is convicted at the crown court of an offence for which an adult could be sentenced to 14 years imprisonment or more and the sentence is not fixed, for example, where the maximum is life imprisonment. This applies to robbery, arson, rape, murder and some other offences. In such cases the court can order that the juvenile go to prison for a period of time up to the maximum provided by the law. The court has to be satisfied that there is no other available method of dealing with the person concerned.

Custody for life

A person under 21 can only be sentenced to life imprisonment if they are convicted of murder. A person aged between 17 and 20 can also be sentenced to life if they are convicted of other offences such as arson, robbery or rape, for which the penalty is life.

A person convicted of murder who is under 18 when the offence was committed cannot be sentenced to life imprisonment but must be sentenced to be detained at Her Majesty's Pleasure (see page 187). In practice there is not much difference between the two sentences.

Compensation orders

A court can order someone to pay compensation instead of imposing another sentence or can make a compensation order on top of any other sentence. The amount is limited to £2,000. Before making an order the court has to consider whether the child or young person can pay. Compensation is payable to the victim of the crime.

The court must order that any compensation be paid by the parent unless the parent cannot be found or it would be unreasonable to do so. Before making such an order the court must give the parent an opportunity to be heard by the court.

Costs

The court has the power to order that the child pay the costs of bringing the case to court. As in the case of fines and compensation orders, the court must order that the parent pay the costs unless it would be unreasonable to make that order or the parent cannot be found. An order for costs cannot be more than the level of any fine imposed.

Growing Up

Few would disagree that a newborn baby is incapable of looking after itself or of making decisions about its life. But as children grow older they acquire more and more of the attributes society feels are needed to make sensible and informed decisions. To some extent the law recognizes this process by gradually extending the range of things a child can do. However, the law has never been thought out clearly. The result is that children acquire rights in a haphazard way throughout their childhood. Although a person is said to have become an adult at the age of 18 and has by then acquired most of the legal rights of an adult, young people still have to wait until they are 21 for some of the rights that adults have.

This section sets out rights that children acquire at different ages. Much criticism is levelled at the illogicality of what follows. Why, for example, should a person be able to marry at 16 but not vote until they are 18? What is the justification for making it possible for a boy to commit rape at 14 but not allow a girl to legally consent to sexual intercourse until she is 16? Although it will always be difficult to decide when children are old enough for specific rights there can be no justification for the present hotchpotch of legislation. Reform is long overdue.

The ages at which rights are acquired

At birth

Children have a number of rights from the moment they are born. They can, for example, make certain kinds of contracts (see page 109). They are entitled to hold a full passport.

A child, from birth, can have a deposit account with some banks or building societies or hold, but not buy, premium bonds. In theory a child can borrow money at birth but as it is unlikely that the borrower could recover the money (see page 111) until the child is 18, borrowing is a difficult business for a child.

A child is liable to be taxed on income from birth in the same way as an adult.

At the age of five

The most significant event that occurs when a child becomes five is that he or she reaches compulsory school age and must either go to school or receive alternative full-time education. This also obliges parents to ensure that their child receives proper education.

Outside London a child aged five can see a 'U' or 'PG' category film at a cinema without an adult being present. In London the age at which this is allowed is seven. Cinema managers, however, always have the right to refuse admission.

A child can drink alcohol in private.

Normally a child aged five will have to pay child's fares on trains, buses, tubes, although this can vary slightly from area to area.

At the age of seven

A child can open and draw money from a National Savings Bank account and a Trustee Savings Bank account.

At the age of 10

A child can be convicted of a criminal offence. However, until the child is 14 the prosecution has to prove that the child knew the difference between right and wrong.

A child can be arrested and detained by the police. In certain circumstances the police have the power to search, take fingerprints, take photographs and samples from the child.

At the age of 12

A child can buy a pet without an adult being present.

At the age of 13

A child can get a part-time job subject to the restrictions imposed by the law (see Chapter 7).

At the age of 14

A child can be convicted of a crime without the additional safeguard provided for children between the ages of 10 and 14 (see above).

A boy can be convicted of rape, assault with intent to commit rape and unlawful sexual intercourse with a girl under 16.

A boy can be sentenced to detention centre.

A child found guilty of an imprisonable offence can be made the subject of a care order.

A child can be given or lent an air weapon, a firearm or ammunition if in possession of a firearm's certificate.

A child can go into a pub to play dominoes or cribbage and drink soft drinks. Buying or drinking alcohol in a pub is still prohibited.

A child has to pay full fare on British Rail.

At the age of 15

A child convicted of a criminal offence can be sentenced to youth custody.

A boy can be sent to prison under certain circumstances to await trial (see page 178).

A child can open a Post Office Girobank account but has to have a guarantor, that is someone who will be liable for any debts incurred.

A child can see a Category 15 film unaccompanied.

A child can have a shotgun if he or she also has a shotgun certificate. The child must either be supervised by someone over 21 or the gun must be in a securely fastened gun cover.

At the age of 16

The most important right won at this age is the right to leave school. Once a child has left school they can work full time and can get a National Insurance number, although their employment in certain jobs is still subject to controls (see Chapter 7).

A young person can claim supplementary benefit.

A young person can join most trade unions. Some can be joined by people aged under 16.

A young person can marry with parental consent or the consent of the court.

A young person can consent or refuse consent to surgical, medical or dental treatment. Prior to 16 a young person will normally have to give consent through his or her parents (but see page 19).

A young person can apply for his or her own passport with the consent of one parent (see page 139) and loses the ability to travel on a parent's passport.

Legal advice and assistance is available under the Green Form legal aid scheme. A young person can apply for legal aid.

A boy can join the armed forces with parental consent.

Young people can buy cigarettes, tobacco and cigarette papers.

A young person aged 16 can have beer, cider or wine with a meal in a restaurant, or room used for meals in a pub or hotel.

Young people can buy liqueur chocolates, fireworks and premium bonds.

A young person can go into a pub without an adult—but not buy alcoholic drinks.

They have to pay full fare on trains, buses and tubes in London.

If convicted of an imprisonable offence, a person can be sentenced to a community service order.

Young people can take part in a public performance without the need for a local authority licence (see page 102).

They can sell scrap metal.

They can go into a brothel and live there.

They can hold a licence to drive a moped, invalid carriage, pedestrian controlled vehicle or mowing machine.

They can probably leave home without consent of a parent or guardian. This is subject to the intervention of the courts, either through care proceedings or wardship proceedings.

Girls can legally consent to sexual intercourse.

At the age of 17

A young person will be tried in a magistrates' court or crown court for a criminal offence.

A young person can be made the subject of a probation order, and, if male, can be sent to prison if convicted of a serious offence.

A young person cannot be received into care (see page 55).

A young person can hold a licence to drive most vehicles except for heavy goods vehicles.

A young person can put his or her name on the electoral register but not vote.

A girl can join the armed forces with parental consent at $17\frac{1}{2}$.

A young person can apply for a helicopter licence and can hold a pilot's licence to fly a private plane.

A young person can have an air weapon in a public place.

A young person can buy or hire any firearm or ammunition as long as he or she has a firearms certificate.

A young person can become a street trader.

At the age of 18

For most purposes young people become adults when they reach the age of 18. They can vote in general and local elections and serve on a jury.

They can own land, buy land, sue and be sued in their own right and administer a dead person's estate.

They can apply for a passport without their parents' consent and can change their name without their parents' consent.

They can open a bank account or Post Office Girobank account iin their own right.

They can make a will.

They can serve on a jury.

They can buy drink and alcohol in a bar and drink in a bar.

They can work in a bar serving drinks.

They can hold a licence to drive a goods vehicle up to 7.5 tonnes.

They can go into a sex shop.

They can enter a betting shop, place a bet and work in a betting shop. They can go to bingo.

They can pawn goods.

They can be tattooed.

They can be blood donors.

Young men and women can join the armed forces without the consent of parents.

A child who is adopted acquires the right to see his or her original birth certificate on application to the Registrar General (see page 51).

Young people cannot be adopted after they have reached the age of 18.

They can see a Category 18 film and buy video recordings with an adult classification (R18).

They will have to pay for dental treatment unless in full-time education, pregnant, or exempt in other ways (see Chapter 9).

A person aged 18 who was a ward of court ceases to be one and can no longer be made one.

A young person ceases to be in care unless he or she was over 16 when the care order was made.

At the age of 21

Young people can become an MP or local councillor.

They can apply for a licence to sell alcohol.

They can hold a licence to drive a large passenger or heavy goods vehicle.

A man can consent to a homosexual act in private without breaking the law if both he and his partner are over 21. Gay relationships between women are not illegal at any age (but see page 161).

A person can adopt a child.

Useful Addresses

CHILDREN'S LEGAL CENTRE

20 Compton Terrace
London N1 2U9
(01) 359 6251

The Children's Legal Centre provides advice and assistance on all
aspects of children's law. It sometimes takes up individual cases
on behalf of children and can often advise a young person about
getting legal help. It campaigns on issues relating to children and
publishes a magazine called *Childright* which deals with the law
affecting children.

NATIONAL ASSOCIATION OF YOUNG PEOPLE IN CARE
(NAYPIC)

9 Southbrook Terrace
Bradford BD7 1AD
(0274) 393938

London Office:

20 Compton Terrace
London N1 2U9
(01) 359 6251

Exists to help young people in care and to campaign for better
treatment for those in care.

CHILD POVERTY ACTION GROUP (CPAG)

1 Macklin Street
London WC2B 5NH
(01) 242 9149/3225

Gives advice on all matters concerning supplementary benefits.
Publishes guides to the benefits system and campaigns for a better
deal for those claiming benefit.

THE GENERAL REGISTER OFFICE
ADOPTED CHILDREN REGISTER

Segensworth Road
Titchfield
Fareham
Hampshire PO15 5RR

Keeps records from which an adopted child over 18 may be able
to trace his or her natural parents.

BRITISH AGENCIES FOR ADOPTION & FOSTERING
(BAAF)

11 Southwark Street
London SE1 1RQ
(01) 407 8800

Assists those wishing to adopt children.

PARENT TO PARENT INFORMATION ON ADOPTION
SERVICES (PPIAS)

Lower Boddington
Daventry
Northants NN11 6YB
(0327) 60295

Publishes newsletter with details of children waiting for adoption.
Puts prospective and existing adopters in touch with each other.

NATIONAL ORGANISATION FOR COUNSELLING
ADOPTEES AND THEIR PARENTS (NORCAP)

49 Russell Hill Road
Purley
Surrey CR2 2XB
(01) 660 4794

Advises adopted people who wish to trace their natural parents.
But does not trace them. It holds a register listing adopted people
and natural parents who wish to make contact.

ADVISORY CENTRE FOR EDUCATION (ACE)

18 Victoria Park Square
London E2 9PB
(01) 980 4596

Advises those involved with state education. Publishes a bi-monthly bulletin and various specific guides.

INDEPENDENT SCHOOLS INFORMATION SERVICE

56 Buckingham Gate
London SW1E 6AG
(01) 630 8793

Advises on school choice in the private sector.

EDUCATION OTHERWISE

25 Common Lane
Hemingford Abbots
Cambridgeshire PE18 9AN
(0480) 63160

Self-help organization offering support, advice and information to families wishing to educate their children at home. Publishes a newsletter and produces a booklet called 'School is not compulsory'.

SOLICITORS FAMILY LAW ASSOCIATION (SFLA)

154 Fleet Street
London EC4A 2HX
(01) 353 3290

Association of lawyers, specializing in family law who try to adopt a conciliatory approach to issues involving family disputes. Can recommend specialist solicitors.

HEALTH AND SAFETY EXECUTIVE

Baynard's House
1 Chepstow Place
London W2 4TF
(01) 229 3456

Has responsibility for enforcing some of the regulations concerning children and employment.

NATIONAL COUNCIL FOR CIVIL LIBERTIES (NCCL)

21 Tabard Street
London SE1 4LA
(01) 403 3888

Gives advice on the law concerning all civil liberties issues and
can take up cases on behalf of individuals. Publishes a wide range
of books and information sheets many of which concern children.

COMMISSION FOR RACIAL EQUALITY

Elliot House
10–12 Allington Street
London SW1E 5EH
(10) 828 7022

EQUAL OPPORTUNITIES COMMISSION

Overseas House
Quay Street
Manchester 3
(061) 833 9244

THE LAW SOCIETY

The Law Society Hall
113 Chancery Lane
London WC2A 1PL
(01) 242 1222

JOINT COUNCIL FOR THE WELFARE OF IMMIGRANTS
(JCWI)

115 Old Street
London EC1V 9JR
(01) 251 8706

Gives advice on the whole range of immigration and nationality
law and can provide representation at immigration appeals.

UNITED KINGDOM IMMIGRANTS ADVISORY SERVICE
(UKAIS)

7th Floor
Brettenham House
Savoy Street
London WC2
(01) 240 5176

Gives advice and assistance to people whose status is threatened
under the immigration legislation.

Index